EUROSTAR

EUROSTAR

SIMON PIELOW

IAN ALLAN *Publishing*

Dedications

I would like to thank my companion in La Quincaillerie restaurant in Brussels for her encouragement and inspiration.
I am also grateful to my children for aspiring to university education – the original impetus for the book!

Front Cover: The dramatic lines of a TMST under the spectacular roof at Waterloo International.

Rear cover upper: Eurostar set Nos 3018/3017 passes through Tonbridge on 29 July 1995 with the 12.27 Waterloo-Brussels service. *A. R. Guppy*

Rear cover lower: Eurostar — a service for passengers of all ages.

Previous pages: Eurostar — the personification of the new age of rail.

Right: Class 373 Eurostar No 3206 at Paris. *BM*

First published 1997

ISBN 0 7110 2451 0

Published by Ian Allan Publishing

an imprint of Ian Allan Ltd, Terminal House, Station Approach, Shepperton, Surrey TW17 8AS.
Printed by Ian Allan Printing Ltd at its works at Coombelands in Runneymede, England.

Code: 9709/B2

Contents

Acknowledgements

The author would like to thank: Simon Forty for writing Chapters 1, 2, 3 and 6; Jonathan Forty for writing Chapter 5 and the Chronology; Peter Waller for writing Chapter 4; Brian Tomlinson for Appendix 2, the Technical Specification; and Alan Butcher for the design.
Others who provided photographs and assistance were:
Alex Obradovic, Richard Wood, Jim Abbott editor of *Modern Railways*, Ken Cordner and, especially, Brian Morrison.
My thanks to all of them.

Photo Credits

All photographs and images in the book, unless individually credited, were provided via the author and are copyright. Those credited BM are by Brian Morrison and those credited IAL are from the Ian Allan Library.

Abbreviations

BR	British Railways
DB	German National Railways
ECML	East Coast main line (Britain)
EPS	European Passenger Services
ICE	German InterCity Express
IECC	Integrated Electronic Control Centre (signalling)
LCR	London & Continental Railways
LGV	Ligne à Grande Vitesse (French high-speed line)
NoL	North of London
SNCB	Belgian National Railways
SNCF	French National Railways
TGV	Train à Grande Vitesse (French high-speed train)
UIC	International Union of Railways. While most of Britain and the Continent use the same track gauge, the loading gauge is different, the Continent working to the UIC or 'Berne' gauge which is bigger than the British one.
WCML	West Coast main line (Britain)

Left: The sleek lines of the Eurostar Transmanche Super Train (TMST) have brought state-of-the-art railway technology to Britain's Railways. At quarter of a mile in length, these impressive trains are longer than any other passenger train in the UK; with the future of the Channel Link bringing high-speed rail travel to the UK, Britain will soon have a railway to rival those of its near neighbours on the Continent.
Alex Dasi-Sutton

Overleaf: Dover castle looks down on the inner harbour in days of steam, as a 'B4' dock tank shunts wagons. *IAL*

Chapter 1

History

History

During the last Ice Age a Channel Tunnel would not have been needed: Britain was part of north-western Europe and early Palaeolithic hunter-gatherers were able to reach England by a land bridge across the Strait of Dover. During the Mesolithic period, about 8,000 years ago, the land bridge was eroded away by the persistent waves of the North Sea as melting glaciers at the end of the Ice Age raised the sea level: Britain became an island again.

The loss of the land bridge did not stop communications with Europe; despite the water barrier, Britain was still part of the European world. We know that there were continued waves of settlers from Europe to Britain — during the later Stone Age and early Bronze Age came the Beaker People who would raise such puzzling megalithic monuments as Stonehenge and Avebury; there was also trade in copper and tin with the Phoenicians from the far-distant eastern Mediterranean. Celtic-speaking immigrants brought iron-working techniques to Britain around 450BC; and later still the Romans brought a measure of modern civilisation. After brief incursions by Julius Caesar in 55BC and 54BC, the Romans actually conquered Britain in AD43, and from then onwards established a rule of force which lasted until the 5th century. Once the Roman Empire weakened and could no longer defend Britain, the Channel was no more than an inconvenience to waves of invading Angles, Saxons and Danes.

Above: Dover Western Docks station provided passengers with easy access between train and ferry. On 15 July 1979 4VEP No 7854 leaves the station with the 12.15 to Victoria. *Les Bertram*

In 1066 the Channel was crossed for the last time by a successful invader: William the Bastard, Duke of Normandy, took England from the Anglo-Saxon Harold Godwinson. The Anglo-French Empire which developed reached its apogee under Henry II, whose lands stretched far south, almost to the Spanish border. The Bordeaux area, today served by SNCF's TGVs, remained in English hands for many years and it would only be in the 16th century during the reign of Queen Mary that England's final possession in France — Calais — was reluctantly surrendered to the French crown.

The rivalry between France and England which had been punctuated by military conflicts like the 100 Years War (1337-1453) and the wars against Napoleon (1803-15) finished in military terms at Waterloo. The peace which followed Napoleon's defeat saw the growth of European tourism, as fashionable people could travel freely around the Continent to examine works of antiquity on the 'Grand Tour'. The great names of foreign travel come from this period: Karl Baedeker lived from 1801-59 and Thomas Cook started his travel tour business in 1863 by organising a trip to Switzerland; he had invented travellers' cheques by the early 1870s.

The growth of traffic to and from England's south coast was accelerated by the invention of the steam engine. This would revolutionise not just land-based travel — within 50 years of the opening of the Stockton to Darlington Railway in 1825 there were many thousands of miles of track in England — but also sea travel. The advent of the cross-Channel steamer in the 1870s and 1880s, much more reliable than the earlier paddleboats, made timetabled services possible and soon the railway companies were running ferry services, taking passengers from London to the Continent via Dover, Folkestone, Newhaven and other south coast ports. This period culminated in the Entente Cordiale — a 1904 agreement between the British and French governments which regularised their colonial disputes and heralded improved relations which would see both countries fighting together against Germany in World War 1.

Immediately after the Great War another mechanical revolution took place. Their technology developed and accelerated by four years of war, aircraft reached a level of safety

Eurostar

Left: Postwar there was a short-lived ferry service for cars by Bristol 170 Freighter. Carrying only two or three cars, it did not catch on. These Bristol Freighters are pictured at Filton. *IAL*

and efficiency that enabled passenger operations to start in earnest. The first daily flights from London to Paris began from Hounslow in June 1919 and in the 1920s and 1930s services increased from London's first designated airport — Croydon.

These air services owed much to the railways — in this period the Great Western, London & North Eastern, London, Midland & Scottish and Southern Railways. From 21 March 1931 Railway Air Services Ltd — a joint venture between these 'Big Four' railway companies and Imperial Airways — started flying operations and fostered the growth of air activity throughout Britain. At the same time, in 1931, car ferry services opened.

While planes could not seriously compete with rail-ferry operations for some years, journey times and prices steadily improved so that flying soon become a viable method of getting across the Channel to European destinations. During this period, in 1936, train ferry terminals opened at Dover and Dunkirk to allow the transit of railway vehicles including a night sleeper service to Paris (this lasted through to 1980).

Left: For many years a Hovercraft service has crossed the Channel successfully, its main drawbacks being the limited number of cars it can carry and the service's cancellation in rough weather. *IAL*

The growth of traffic figures continued after World War 2 with different principals: British nationalisation of air and railway companies created British Railways and British European Airways, later to become part of British Airways. The ferries meanwhile were controlled by the British Transport Commission (Southern Region) which became the British Transport Board in 1963 and Sealink from 1979. From an early date ferry operations were linked to French railways — from 1862 the Société de Chemin de Fer de l'Ouest; from 1909 the Société de Chemin de Fer de l'État and from 1936 the Société Nationale des Chemins de Fer Français — SNCF.

The increased passenger and freight business exploded in the 1970s, aided by Britain's joining the EEC in 1973 and then again when the single European market was created in 1992, taking away quotas and tariffs between participating countries. The importance of European trading partners and the necessity of easy physical communications made it natural to look again at creating a closer and quicker travel link with the Continent than that afforded by air travel — always expensive for freight — and the ferries — inherently time-consuming.

Thus it was in 1973 that an Anglo-French treaty on trial tunnel borings was signed. Although this was cancelled in 1975 because of escalating costs and a change of government, it was not long — six years — before the sheer volume of cross-Channel movements forced the idea to the political forefront again: by the start of the 1990s nearly 50 million people were crossing the Channel each way annually— more than three times the 1970s figure. The method of linking the two countries was yet again discussed in detail: as before, the weather, the heavy sea traffic between Dover and Calais and the distance all militated against a bridge. So it was that in 1986 the plan proposed by the Channel Tunnel consortium was adopted and an Anglo-French treaty was signed. It was ratified in 1987 and construction of the Channel Tunnel started in November of that year.

Below: The night ferry was a popular way of getting to the Continent. Here sleeping cars go into the *St Germain* for the Channel crossing from Dover to Dunkerque. *IAL*

Above: Inside the car deck of a Southern Railway ferry. Note the train rails on the decking. *IAL*

Left: A French loco prepares to haul out coaches from a train ferry. *IAL*

15

The Tunnel

The idea of a tunnel had first been mooted way back in 1751 when a French farmer, Nicolas Desmaret, suggested a fixed link across the Channel. A second attempt in 1802 by the engineer Albert Mathieu-Favier saw discussions between the two sides scuppered by Napoleon's ambitions and the resumption of a war between the two countries which would last for over a decade. In the spirit of Anglo-French hostility and misunderstandings, it would have been strange to countenance a fixed link!

There was another abortive attempt by Joseph-Aimé Thomé de Gamond who proposed to lay iron tubes on the seafloor in the 1830s and who even got as far as making extensive investigations of the seabed. Then in 1867 two Englishmen, William Low and Sir John Clarke Hawkshaw, proposed a tunnel and set up the Channel Tunnel Co in 1872. Their tunnel advanced 1.85km from Shakespeare Cliff before it failed, and it was left to the politicians to sign the Anglo-French Protocol of 1876, perhaps encouraged by the new-found optimism of a stable — and friendly — Fourth Republic. Unfortunately, the tunnel begun by Sir William Watkin and Alexandre Levalley in 1881 managed only 4km before being stopped by the British in 1882: the main reason being the paranoia of British public opinion which feared a French invasion through the tunnel.

The Entente Cordiale led to another scheme in 1904 for a twin tunnel; this and two attempts to put a bill before the House in 1907 and 1930 foundered. During the 1960s and 1970s the idea kept resurfacing but it was only in the 1980s that the time, the technology and the

Above: The real thing: a view of the lower Shakespeare Cliff site in February 1989. From this point the British tunnels, both landward and seaward, were constructed. *Eurotunnel*

politics were all ready to provide the commitment needed to see the job through. Following studies launched in September 1981 as to its feasibility, the construction and running of the Channel Tunnel was put out to tender in 1985. On 20 January 1986 Margaret Thatcher and François Mitterrand announced the winner of the competition: the victorious consortium was the France Manche-Channel Tunnel Group, which quickly evolved into Eurotunnel. It was the only tender to involve an exclusively rail solution to the tunnel, the other three bidders had combined road and rail operations. The concession granted required Eurotunnel to build and operate the tunnel for 30 years.

Immediately the winner was announced, discussions were undertaken between the consortium and the railways (SNCF and BR) to work out a contract for rail use; this took 18 months to sort out and during this time the necessary agreements and requirements had to be put in to law on both sides of the Channel. The French insisted, rightly, that high speed had to be part of the contract; and with their experience of existing TGV operations, they were well placed to deliver high speed running over new track.

In Britain on 23 July 1987 the Channel Tunnel Act received Royal Assent. The act was particularly noteworthy for its specific lack of state funding for the project. In fact the British Government is barred from giving grants towards the provision of international services. The Treaty of Canterbury was ratified on 29 July 1987. BR's involvement would be handled by the new European Passenger Services operation.

The Eurotunnel contract with the railways identified four main users of the tunnel which would become:

- **Eurostar** — the brand name for the high speed passenger service connecting London, Brussels and Paris which would be run by European Passenger Services (EPS), SNCF and SNCB

- **Rail Freight** — the organisation operated by British and French railway companies to carry freight

17

- **Le Shuttle Freight** — Eurotunnel's freight vehicle service between Folkestone and Calais
- **Le Shuttle** — Eurotunnel's vehicle service carrying cars, motorcycles and their passengers

The Channel Tunnel, the sole fixed link between the UK and France, is actually three tunnels: two running tunnels plus a service tunnel between them for maintenance and emergency access. Eurotunnel employed a joint venture of 10 UK and French construction companies called TransManche Link (TML) to build the tunnel. The joint venture partners were Balfour Beatty, Costain, Tarmac, Taylor Woodrow and Wimpey of UK and SAE, SGE, Spie Batignolles, Bouygues and Dumez of France. TML's UK-based member companies undertook that part of the construction which was located primarily in the UK and the France-based companies undertook construction on the French side.

The construction brief was not just for the tunnel itself; TML had to construct the two terminals on either side of the Channel, at Folkestone and Coquelles, as well as organising the design and manufacture of Le Shuttle trains — altogether one of the biggest civil construction jobs of the century. It is not surprising to learn that, at the peak of construction, TML employed over 15,000 personnel and was spending £4 million a day!

It has to be said that the technical tunnelling difficulties were more to do with the size and complexity of the operation rather than extreme conditions. For example, while the Seikan Tunnel in Japan (which takes Japanese Railways' Shinkansen bullet train) is longer at 54km, the Channel Tunnel is amongst the largest complex of tunnels ever built — 149km of bored tunnel in total. The tunnel was excavated through a bed of almost watertight homogeneous chalk marl on the UK side which made for straightforward work although the fractured, water-bearing folded strata on the French side were a little more complicated and did cause problems.

The Channel Tunnel statistics are impressive: at their deepest point, the tunnels are 130m below sea level and 75m below the seabed. The diameter of the two running tunnels is 7.6m, that of the service tunnel 4.8m. Link passages 3.3m in diameter every 375m were constructed

Right: Assembly of the the second (south seaward) running tunnel boring machine in February 1989. *Eurotunnel*

Left: Communications tests in the tunnel.
TRL Technology

between the running tunnels and the central service tunnel. Piping totalling 450km in length and requiring 100,000 fixing brackets and supports was installed in them. The electrical power needed to run the trains and the tunnel facilities is enormous — for the trains alone in excess of 160MW (a smallish city with 250,000 inhabitants would use this at peak times). The catenaries to supply the trains include 950km of overhead conductor cables; they probably have the highest rating in the world with a current-carrying capacity of 2,500A. In the tunnels and terminals nearly 15,000 supports were needed. 20,000 light fittings were installed in the tunnels alone and 1,300km of cable was required to distribute power underground.

The surveying, too, had to be of pinpoint accuracy to ensure a satisfactory mid-Channel join. Compensation was even made for the refraction caused by differing densities of the cold air against the wall compared with the warmer air at the centre line. This ensured that the first tunnel to meet (the service tunnel) was accurate to within 500mm.

The hard work started on 15 December 1987 and was done by 11 tunnel-boring machines — TBMs. There were six on the UK side and five on the French. The UK machines were all built in Britain and were lowered in pieces down a shaft 110m deep and 10m in internal diameter and rebuilt in an erection chamber. The larger of the machines weighed 1,350 tonnes and cost an average of £7 million each. Amazingly, as they were not expected to be used again, several were left in the ground and concreted over because the expense of lifting and storing them was too high. The TBMs on the French side were launched from an open access shaft 75m deep and 55m in diameter. The maximum total rate of progress sustained over a six-month period was 1.5km each month.

At the one-third and two-thirds points the running tunnels were designed to enter submarine caverns, constructed to permit trains to cross from one running tunnel to the other and so to allow operations during tunnel maintenance. These caverns are remarkable, the largest of their sort ever to have been excavated under the sea: each is 164m long by 21m wide and 15m high.

The tunnels themselves are lined with approximately 800,000 precast concrete segments which fitted together make up a circular ring. These weigh between one tonne and nine tonnes and were placed by the TBMs as they advanced. The UK segments were manufactured in a special casting yard at the Isle of Grain in Kent. The high quality granite aggregate used was imported by sea from the 'superquarry' at Glensanda on Loch Leven near Fort William in Scotland. To minimise road traffic movements these segments and the

Right: Assembly in the tunnel workings of the huge cutter-head of the first running tunnel boring machine in November 1988.

majority of other construction materials were brought from the Isle of Grain by rail to a purpose-built railhead covering 57 hectares at Sevington near Ashford, Kent.

Excavated material from each side of the tunnels amounted to about 4.3 million cubic metres. This was removed from the tunnel by narrow-gauge diesel-hauled railcars, deposited in a bunker at the bottom of the access shaft and then taken to the surface by conveyor. On the UK side it was then deposited in a 25-hectare rectangular lagoon to form reclaimed land for storage and a range of temporary site facilities. To form the lagoon, one side of which was the original coastline, a sea wall 1,700m long was constructed using steel sheet piles. The weight of piles driven, between September 1987 and December 1990, was 32,500 tonnes. Rock

weighing a total 60,000 tonnes was placed at the foot of the seaward face of the sea wall in order to protect it against scour. This was one of the world's largest sheet pile undertakings.

The key mechanical systems in the tunnel were identified by TML as:

- **Drainage** — two pumping stations on either side of the tunnel can empty each bore in half an hour
- **Fire-fighting** — a piped water system down the service tunnel can deliver 120 tonnes of water an hour and if all the pumps fail, there is a big enough static head of water for the system to work; all the hydrants are equipped for both French and British equipment

- **Tunnel ventilation** — two systems: the normal which provides fresh air thanks to 2m-diameter fans at each end; and a supplementary system for emergencies
- **Cooling** — without cooling, temperatures in the tunnel would rocket towards a figure possibly as high as 50°C. There are special plants on each coast each equipped with four enormous refrigerators: the largest is equivalent to over 25,000 of the domestic type

The site available for the UK Folkestone terminal — 8km from the tunnel workings at Shakespeare Cliff — was 2.5km long by, at its widest, 900m wide. A volume of 2.6 million cubic metres of sand was pumped a length of 4.2km from the seabed to the UK terminal and placed up to 12m deep in order to level the site which then required a total of 5.5 million cubic metres of earthworks to bring it up to the height necessary to ensure that the Shuttles did not have a stiff gradient to climb. At some points this meant raising the surface by 12m.

The huge site of the French terminal at Coquelles was closer to the French tunnel workings at Sangatte: at its closest 3.25km away. The site was 70 per cent marshland and 15 million cubic metres of earthworks were required, including extra material to squeeze out water from the marsh; it was later removed. The TML statisticians worked this out to be the equivalent of a volume seven times the size of Egypt's largest pyramid, the great pyramid of Cheops. The site also needed excavations up to 30m deep in order to give its required 800m length and ensure that the Shuttles came into the terminal at the correct height. This excavation created the 'Tranché de Beussingue'.

Each terminal includes four multi-span overbridges some 350m long which enable rapid on- and off-loading of road vehicles from the railway shuttles; a number of other bridges (17 in the UK and 11 in France), roads and other paved areas, infrastructure works and several substantial buildings. Between mid-1991 and the end of 1992, block-paved surfacing was placed, 60,000 cubic metres for platforms and ramps and 55,000 cubic metres around buildings and for car parks.

Completed in December 1993, the tunnel stretches 50km from terminal to terminal; the final cost of construction alone was £2,700 million. Total cost including the terminals, rolling stock, etc, was about £7,000 million.

Le Shuttle services depart from each terminal every 15 minutes at peak times with a minimum departure of one an hour. The following are not allowed passage through the tunnel:

- Gas tankers
- Cargoes of liquid petroleum
- Petroleum tankers
- Cargoes of nuclear waste
- Cargoes of dangerous chemicals
- Livestock.

Left : Breakthrough! The cutting crews celebrate.

The Eurostar Service

Impressive though the technology undoubtedly is, the tunnel is but one part of the Eurostar story. Le Shuttle simply carries motor vehicles and their passengers under the Channel from the road network of one country to that of next, where the vehicles continue their onward journeys at a legal maximum speed limit of around 70mph; Eurostar trains reach speeds of 300km/hr as they bullet their way through the countryside on their three capitals service. To travel this quickly requires a highly sophisticated infrastructure dedicated to high speed, with

negotiate agreements for traffic on each other's lines. Once the principles had been agreed, the railways had to set up project groups for the nitty-gritty details of the planning and construction of the infrastructure, the lines, terminals, maintenance depots, and, of course, not forgetting the trains themselves. BR set up EPS in 1991 to develop passenger services using the Channel Tunnel. It became the British partner in Eurostar.

To begin with, the termini were to be constructed at three important, historic locations — Waterloo station in south London, Brussels

Right: It hasn't all been plain sailing: this time the problem was a broken rail. The 10.23 London-Paris service on 3 April 1996 pulls away from a signal stop with the 10.27 Waterloo-Brussels Eurostar visible in the distance held at the next signal back.
Peter J. Howard

new stations, signalling, control centres and all the paraphernalia that goes with the safe conduct of railway operations.

When the Treaty of Canterbury was ratified on 29 July 1987 and everyone's attention was diverted to the digging of the tunnel, the Eurostar consortium — BR, SNCF and SNCB — set up project groups to manage the planning and construction of the railway. The Eurostar services would receive 50 per cent of the tunnel 'pathways' paying Eurotunnel a users' fee. At the same time the railway partners had to

Midi and Paris's Gare du Nord. Each of these had to be located carefully and the Eurostar operations had to be separated — for security reasons — from the rest of the station. Intermediate stations were required at Ashford (Kent), Calais-Fréthun and Lille, while the sites for the maintenance depots were chosen as North Pole, outside Paddington in west London, Le Landy outside Paris and Forest in Brussels. New freight yards were also planned — at Wembley and Dollands Moor in England and Fréthun in France.

Left: At least it's warm inside: Eurostar travelling through winter countryside.

On top of this, the existing lines in the UK had to be readied for use when the tunnel was opened and new lines had to built in Belgium — France already having approved the construction of the new TGV Nord line; the routes selected and the infrastructure — power supply, bridges, viaducts, platforms, etc — improved (see Chapter 2: Infrastructure). The

Below: The front of the Eurostar was designed to be as aerodynamically perfect as possible

trains had to be designed, tested and built — trains which had to be big to maximise loads and financial efficiency through the tunnel; trains which had to solve the complexities of three countries' different power supplies; trains which would have to be driven by crews across international borders to foreign locations under different railways' rules and regulations.

Below: Eurostar Nos 3219/3220 passes the west end of Dollands Moor Yard on the 12.27 Waterloo-Brussels service on 14 February 1995. In the background the French-built two-tier car transporters, coupled together in five-car articulated sets joined by bellow passenger-ways. *Peter J. Howard*

The Trains

The transformation of the vision of a high-speed train service linking London with Paris and Brussels via the Channel Tunnel into reality began on 18 December 1989 when the contract to build what were then known as TransManche Super Trains — TMSTs — was awarded to a consortium of engineering companies, led by GEC-Alsthom. But the story had started before that when the three railway companies set up the International Project Group (IPG). The contract required the design and production of 30 trains for the three railway networks. This contract was later amended (see Chapter 2).

The trains, to be given the branding 'Eurostar', were to be based upon proven technology utilised by the established SNCF fleet of high-speed TGV passenger trains. Eurostar was to differ, however, through increased length — and thereby, crucially, seating capacity — and a smaller cross-section (known as 'structural loading gauge') to permit operation in Great Britain.

The train was required to be compatible with the infrastructure of each of the three countries, which includes the capability to operate from three different electrical power supply voltages and over five different signalling systems. In

Left: The first solo outing of UK3. Eurostar Nos 3003/4 winds through Factory Junction at Wandsworth Road on 12 February 1994 on a test run from North Pole International to Ashford and back. *BM*

addition, it was also necessary for the train to comply with new stringent safety standards for operation of passenger trains through the Channel Tunnel which includes the ability to split and abandon part of the train in the event of an emergency should this be necessary. More prosaically, it also needed to be able to disgorge its passengers on to three different heights of platform.

These demanding specification requirements coupled with the employment of most modern developments in railway engineering were to make Eurostar one of the most technologically advanced services in Europe.

Left: The first solo outing of UK3. Eurostar Nos 3003/4 winds through Factory Junction at Wandsworth Road on 12 February 1994 on a test run from North Pole International to Ashford and back. *BM*

Below: Following a press call at Waterloo International on 14 February 1994, Eurostar UK3 approaches Vauxhall on its return to North Pole International Depot. The Palace of Westminster is in the background on the extreme left. *BM*

25

The Channel Tunnel Rail Link

The British rail infrastructure from London to the tunnel — despite the upgrading work carried out between 1988 and 1994 — was never going to be able to provide the sort of high-speed service required. It was essential that England — like Belgium and France — got its own dedicated high-speed track. It will do so in the form of the Channel Tunnel Rail Link (CTRL) running a distance of 108km from St Pancras in north central London, to the tunnel — so becoming the first major new railway in Britain for over a century. The actual route is more fully described in Chapter 6.

CTRL brings a series of major benefits :

- It will cut the current journey time to the tunnel portal in half with a projected 35min service (as opposed to today's leisurely 70min). This will reduce the overall London to Paris journey time to about 2hr 30min, and cut that to Brussels to just over two hours — serious competition for the airlines
- Waterloo International's service will join the CTRL just east of Ebbsfleet at a junction near Gravesend and see its overall journey times cut by 15min
- It will enable twice as many trains to run on the Intercapitals service — a projected eight trains an hour
- It will provide an important link for other areas of Britain via the East and West Coast main lines to the Midlands and North (a cut-off direct to the WCML is planned so that through traffic need not move via St Pancras)
- It will provide the track for improved high-speed commuter workings (as is anticipated with the Brussels link) and two new stations — at Stratford, east London and Ebbsfleet, north Kent. It is intended that up to eight trains an hour will use the new line in peak hour periods. This could see London-Dover times cut to 1hr 10min (40min saving), Ashford-London cut by 35min to 40min and Gravesend-London at 20min rather than 50min. 25,000

commuters will benefit and urban regeneration and development anticipated to be worth £500 million should take place. Furthermore it is projected that upwards of 80,000 new jobs will be created by this regeneration

The CTRL has had a chequered history. Involving massive public concern and protests, intense political lobbying and many changes of direction, the story would be unbelievable if it were a novel! In brief, the sequence of events was as follows:

- The Channel Tunnel Treaty sees BR maintaining that no extra rail capacity would be needed for the foreseeable future. By the time the Channel Tunnel Act is passed, BR has accepted extra capacity would be needed by the year 2000, and later that year chooses King's Cross as the likely second terminal. The choice is dictated by the need for north of London services. Various routes are submitted and, following a competition asking for a tender to build, finance and run the link, BR sets up the CTRL team to handle the debate.

  As always in major works of this nature the question of funding is of paramount importance. The Channel Tunnel Act has put precise rules on this but there is a plan to get round the level of public investment by using the rail link for commuter traffic.

  In October 1989 BR plumps for the Eurorail (Trafalgar House) tender and announces in November the European Rail Link; 10,000 march against the link in London. Two of the other consortia — plans put forward by Arup of the Kentrail consortium and US construction company Bechtel — refuse to accept the decision and campaign for alternative approaches.

- In 1990 the Transport Secretary Cecil Parkinson reveals that the government is aware of the level of disquiet which is heightened by the publication in March of Arup's alternative route. After heavy lobbying, Parkinson rejects the BR plan because of the size of public subsidy required. The line goes out to tender again, schemes being presented to new Transport Secretary Malcolm Rifkind in June 1991. In October that year Rifkind announces Ove Arup's route as the preferred option despite intense opposition from BR — in particular Sir Bob Reid, the Chairman, who says that he feels the government's choice is political and not transport-led. Arup joins the Rail Link Project team which then becomes Union Railways, they present their reports, dated March and October 1993, to the government.

- Transport Secretary John MacGregor gives the go-ahead and confirms the route in January 1994 after public consultation. Tendering for construction and operating of the line is reduced to four bidders:

Eurorail, London & Continental Railways, Union Link and a group which becomes Green Arrow.

- At the start of 1995, two months after the Eurostar operation opened, the CTRL Bill has its second reading and a Select Committee begins its deliberations. In April the same year Union Railways joined EPS as a government-owned company, EPS having been taken from BR in April 1994. In July 1995 Eurorail and L&CR are selected for the final stage and the Select Committee, by now in its record-breaking 53rd day of business, makes a variety of recommendations. Its final session takes place on 31 January 1996 after 320 hours and 70 meetings. On 29 February LCR is declared the winner.

Below: A diagram presented to the House of Lords Select Committee while the Channel Tunnel Rail Link Bill was being considered. It shows the projected journey times between the tunnel and London St Pancras.

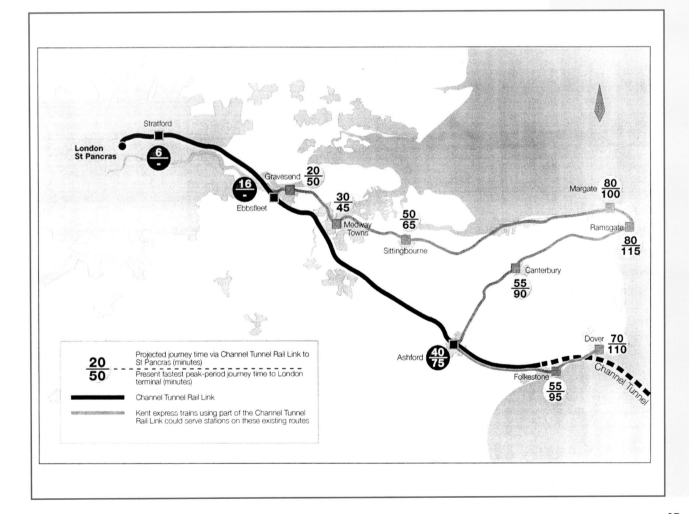

Getting the Line Through

The CTRL is the result of an unprecedented development and refinement process to keep environmental effects to the minimum without compromising safety, operational, engineering and commercial requirements..

- Route alternatives totalled 10 times the length of the 108km railway
- There were over 100 local route variations evaluated
- Union Railways held some 1,700 meetings with members of the public, local authorities and parish councils, MPs, commercial firms, statutory agencies (such as English Heritage, the NRA and Countryside Commission)
- 175 public information centres at 40 separate locations presented detailed information
- 85% of the route is in tunnels or alongside existing transport corridors (motorways, major roads or railways)
- The plans were examined in one of the most comprehensive environmental statements ever produced in this country consisting of 10 volumes backed up by 14 specialist reports
- In the end there will be 60 domestic demolitions — substantially fewer than BR's original southerly route

Below: The trailing end of a Eurostar set passing Sellindge, Kent, while operating the 10.27 Waterloo-Brussels service on 3 April 1996. The photograph gives a clear view of power unit No 3208 and the powered bogie under the first coach.
Peter J. Howard

Left: Eurostar No 3010 leaves Saltwood Tunnel on 31 January 1996 with the 12.27 service from Waterloo to Brussels. *BM*

London & Continental Railways

On 29 February 1996 London & Continental Railways was selected by the British Government as the company to design, build, finance and maintain the CTRL in Britain, linking London via a new high-speed railway line to the tunnel. Announced by the Transport Secretary Sir George Young, the central features of LCR's winning bid were:

- Developing Eurostar services to compete more effectively with airlines until it becomes the profitable market leader
- Making the CTRL directly accessible from the regions throughout Britain
- Close management of the contractors to enable completion of the CTRL on time and within budget
- Design and construction must at least be up to the environmental standards of the 21st century
- Value for money for the taxpayer, guaranteed by real transfer of all financial risk to the private sector
- Taking traffic away from existing lines thereby releasing capacity in the network to carry other services, including international freight

This selection by definition had to include the assumption of ownership of a host of government assets:

- European Passenger Services
- Union Railways
- Eurostar trains
- King's Cross railway land for the new terminal
- Waterloo International
- Ashford International
- North Pole Eurostar maintenance depot
- Regional Eurostar maintenance depot in Manchester
- A site at Kensington Olympia where facilities for border controls and security and train marshalling are being provided
- Certain railway lands at Stratford

LCR has eight shareholders.

- Ove Arup and Partners — the design and planning consultancy which did so much to secure the route. With 2% of the share holding

- Bechtel Ltd — a leading worldwide engineering construction and project management company. 18% of the shares guarantees Bechtel an important role in the project management of the building of the link
- Sir William Halcrow and Partners — a leading British international consulting engineer company. 2% of the shares. Tunnelling experts (useful as 25% of the link is below ground) having worked on the Channel Tunnel and many other railway or underground projects
- National Express Group — one of the UK's leading private sector provider of surface passenger transport. 17% of the shares. With massive ticketing experience it has all-round knowledge of transport company takeovers (it took over West Midlands Travel — buses — and also runs East Midlands and Bournemouth airports)
- Virgin Group Ltd — a subsidiary of Virgin with particular strengths in the business travel market through Britain's second largest scheduled air transport company. With 17% of the shares Virgin brings its considerable expertise in these areas to the company
- SBG Warburg — international investment bank with 18% of the shares — the money men
- Systra — worldwide project managers and consultants with extensive high-speed rail experience. 14% of the shares. Born from the merger of French railway engineering departments of SNCF and Métro operator RATP, they make perfect partners because of their extensive knowledge of TGV and rail operations
- London Electricity — prime suppliers and distributors of electricity in London with 12% of the shares

Chaired by Sir Derek Hornby, LCR's avowed intent is to develop a major, fully integrated transportation company. This means realising the full potential of both international and domestic travel markets and the complete exploitation of all related business

Below: Early morning sun illuminates the 07.13 Paris-Waterloo service as it approaches Willesborough level crossing in Ashford, Kent at 08.20 on 2 February 1995. *Peter J. Howard*

opportunities. It has pledged a new railway designed and constructed to the environmental standards presented to Parliament and completed on time and on budget.

The actual organisation that oversees the construction of the CTRL is its subsidiary Union Railways; the project will be designed and managed on behalf of Union Railways under contract by London & Continental Engineering — a joint venture set up by Bechtel, Arup, Halcrow and Systra. The infrastructure will also be marketed in much the same way that Railtrack markets the ex-BR lines by Pathways, part of Union Railways.

At last after many years of trying, Britain is set to have a high-speed link with the Continent. The Bill authorising the CTRL received Royal Ascent in December 1996. But the story isn't over yet: still to come is the fundraising by London & Continental to pay for the construction work. Construction and commissioning will take five and a half years — with the time-critical elements being the London tunnels (about 20km of underground working), St Pancras, the trackwork and electrical and control systems.

Below: Eurostar Nos 3216/5 passes Vauxhall en route for North Pole International Depot on 25 November 1994. *Chris Wilson*

Overleaf: An aerial view of Waterloo station and the completed International Terminal, its long blue curving roof standing out on the north of the main station building.

31

Infrastructure

The Termini and Stations

Waterloo International, London

Waterloo station may not have been the most tactfully named of termini to be chosen as the English end for trains travelling to and from France; it was, however, the most practicable in the short term until the route of a high-speed link could be organised. Although traditionally trains to the cross-Channel ferries are associated with Victoria, Waterloo could provide the scope for the rebuilding necessary for the construction of the major new international terminal.

Waterloo is the biggest station in the British Isles, occupying a ground area of 10 hectares. Its history dates back to 11 July 1848 when it opened as the London terminus of the London & South Western Railway. It grew rapidly. After many extensions and changes, the muddled complex of platforms and lines was pulled together into one massive station officially opened by Queen Mary on 21 March 1922 — with a splendid pedestrian entrance, now opposite the International Terminal, in the form of the Victory Arch, which also has a memorial to London & South Western Railway staff killed in World War 1.

Waterloo is situated on the 'Surrey' bank of the River Thames close to the South Bank complex which was developed for the Festival of Britain in 1951 but has since been extended. The South Bank boasts an impressive collection of artistic and performance locations — the Hayward Gallery, Queen Elizabeth Hall, Purcell Room, National Theatre, National Film Theatre, Museum of the Moving Image and the Royal Festival Hall — with the huge Shell Centre looming over it. Within easy reach of Waterloo Bridge (which crosses the Thames in the direction of Covent Garden) and Westminster Bridge leading past the tower of

Far left: A Eurostar pulls into Waterloo's International Terminal. *Craig and Derricott*

Left: A model of the International Terminal at Waterloo. The passenger waiting area can be seen below the tracks.

Below: Aerial view of Waterloo station while the construction of the International Terminal was under way.
Chorley & Handford Ltd

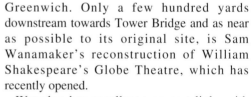

Big Ben to Parliament Square, Waterloo is at the heart of a growing complex of riverfront developments which today is seeing old warehouses and historic sites renovated and rebuilt along the south bank almost to Greenwich. Only a few hundred yards downstream towards Tower Bridge and as near as possible to its original site, is Sam Wanamaker's reconstruction of William Shakespeare's Globe Theatre, which has recently opened.

Waterloo has excellent transport links with central London (Northern and Bakerloo tube lines, black and brown respectively on the maps) as well as offering train services to the south and west of England (mainly Surrey, Sussex, Hampshire and Dorset); its smaller sibling Waterloo East (reached by an escalator from the main station) serves Charing Cross and London Bridge and through them stations in Kent and other destinations in the south-east — including Greenwich. Interestingly Waterloo also boasted — until its recent transfer — the only Underground service in the capital not run by London Transport — the Waterloo & City Line (known to city commuters as the 'Drain') which takes passengers under the Thames to the City of London and its financial institutions.

Far left, top: The concourse at Waterloo International in November 1995 with passengers gathering for the 15.53 to Paris. *Chris Wilson*

Far left, bottom: Checking the roof of the International Terminal entails a longer than expected walk!

Left: I don't fancy yours much! Eurostar Nos 3008/3007 awaits departure at Waterloo International alongside an electric multiple-unit converted for training purposes. *D. Bateman*

The award-winning, purpose-built five-platform international station covers land to the side of Waterloo over what used to be platforms 18 to 21 — hitherto servicing Windsor and Reading. (To compensate for this loss of platforms, two additional platforms were constructed on what was the taxi road.) The 3 hectare site is today covered by one of the most dramatic modern stations anywhere. Designed by Nicholas Grimshaw, perhaps the most striking aspect is the tapering roof, which is constructed from 1 hectare of glass and 0.8 hectare of stainless steel sheeting; it is supported by 37 bowstring arches which vary in span from 48.5m to 32.7m, with an overall length of 400m. The terminal was constructed by Bovis who completed the project on time.

Pushed through by Sir Bob Reid — the Chairman of British Rail, the nationalised railway company that ran Britain's rail network before the privatisation in 1995-7 — the terminal signalled his personal commitment to the Eurostar concept, at a time when the majority of the British public really did not believe that the Channel Tunnel would ever be finished! Sir Bob had been the Chairman of Shell International, and so had come to British Rail at Margaret Thatcher's invitation to modernise the railway. It has to be said that he had been uncertain whether to accept — until his son persuaded him to take up the challenge with the goad that 'Running Shell is easy — BR would be something different!' After privatisation Waterloo station fell into the Railtrack remit along with all Britain's stations and track although Waterloo International is itself owned by London & Continental.

Construction of the International Terminal started in December 1990 and the completed terminal was opened on 6 May 1993 after 30 months' work at a cost of £130 million. It is built on four levels and is entered from the north end of Waterloo station next to the walkway to the Shell building and the Victory Arch. The ticket office, check-in and access point to the Underground network are all at Level 2, just below the tracks which are on the top level: there are five 400m long platforms, sunlit below the massive glass roof. The international concourse and departures hall below the platforms has shops, restaurants, banking services and the Eurostar Clubhouse for Premium First ticket holders and Silver and Gold level members of Eurostar Frequent Traveller with complimentary refreshments and modern office facilities.

The arrivals hall is at ground level, and there is a basement car park for nearly 100 vehicles — apart from those taken up by staff on the earliest shift, these are available for passengers upon payment of a fee. Security, catering, control and the other facilities required to run a secure station are situated from the departures level downwards into the cavernous and

impenetrable corridors 'underneath the arches'.

There was also major work to the Underground station to provide access to the International Terminal and to cope with the fluctuations of traffic occasioned by surges of up to 1,600 passengers (two Eurostar trains) at once.

The author was involved in a function at the ready (but as then unused by trains) Terminal in 1994 when he guided a group up onto a platform. Amongst the guests was a bow-tied man wearing pink-rimmed spectacles. The author enquired whether the man had visited the terminal before and was told he had. And what did he think of it? It was fine. And who was he? The architect, Nicholas Grimshaw!

Gare du Nord, Paris

With 500,000 passengers a day, Gare du Nord is not only the busiest station in France but also in Europe — and third in the world after Chicago and Tokyo. The 1995 annual passenger figure of 21 million is anticipated to rise to 36 million in 1997. As well as being the French terminus for Eurostar operations, it is also the terminus for another major international railway project — the Thalys. This joint venture between Dutch, Belgian, French, and ultimately German railways, the Thalys opened in June 1996 and links Paris, Amsterdam and Cologne via Brussels and Liège. It stops at Mons, Brussels Anvers, Rotterdam, La Haye, Schiphol airport and Amsterdam on one leg and via Brussels on the other to Liège. In the future a high speed line will link up to Aachen and Cologne. The trains themselves are TGVs painted in a distinctive and eye-catching red and grey.

Gare du Nord sees 1,300 train movements a day from its 28 platforms, including those serving the Grandes Lignes — main line trains including the TGV Nord services which opened in May 1993 to Dunkirk, Arras, Cambrai, Calais and Boulogne — from the main hall, as well as local trains from la Gare des Banlieue — the station situated above the Métro and RER stations. It serves the Île-de-France region, to the east and north of Paris

Above: Passengers take the escalator down to their waiting train at Gare du Nord.

Below: Hitorff's impressive frontage of the Gare du Nord in Paris.

Above: Eurostar lineup at Paris Nord on 6 March 1996, from left to right the 07.53 from Waterloo, the 13.07 to Waterloo and the 08.23 from Waterloo. *BM*

through St Denis. The RER station carries Line B (blue on the maps) from Robinson to (B2) and St Rémy-les-Chevreuse (B4) to Roissy/ Charles de Gaulle (B3) and Mitry-Claye (B5) and Line D (green) from Orry-la-Ville to Châtelet-les-Halles. The Métro lines which serve Gare du Nord are: 2 — Nation to Porte Dauphine via Père Lachaise cemetery and Charles de Gaulle Étoile, the station for the Arc de Triomphe; 4 — Porte de Clignancourt to Porte d'Orléans via Cité, Châtelet-les-Halles and Gare de l'Est; 5 — Bobigny-Pablo Picasso

Right: Forward travel into France is easy from the Eurostar terminus as the Métro and RER services are just a short walk away.

to Place d'Italie via Bastille, République and Gare de l'Est.

The station itself was opened on 19 April 1864 for Baron James de Rothschild, president of the Compagnie du Chemin de Fer du Nord, taking over from a previous 1846 station. Built in four years by architect Jacques Hittorff (it was finally finished in 1865), the station has a wonderful, imposing façade, 180m long, made of stone quarried from the Oise valley. At the top are nine statues by Cavelier symbolising the principal cities the station was intended to serve, including at the centre and larger than the others, the city of Paris. The story goes that the reason this façade cannot be properly admired and seen better is that Hittorff was on bad terms with Baron Haussmann, Prefect of the Seine and therefore responsible for roads in and around Paris. The baron made sure that Hittorff's masterpiece could not be seen properly from any vantage point to show off its magnificence. Its 36,000sq m area includes the main hall which has a height of 70m and whose columns were built in Glasgow.

In the 1990s with Eurostar and TGV operations in mind, the interior was renovated with sweeping changes to the great hall which contains the Grandes Lignes. Part of an SNCF programme which included the construction of high-speed lines to Lille Europe, Roissy/Charles de Gaulle, Chessy/Marne-la-Vallée and Satolas, work started in January 1990 and three years later in May 1993 the first TGV Nord entered the station.

The Gare Londres — the Eurostar terminal — was built on a specially constructed mezzanine floor which runs around two sides of the station. It was inaugurated on the same day as Waterloo — 6 May 1994; it shares other similarities with Waterloo — for example the style of seating in the waiting areas. Built within the existing station, the terminal blends well with its august surroundings and has four dedicated platforms. Unfortunately access and waiting area are both more difficult than they need be. Underground parking gives 1,300 spaces (and, incidentally, accounted for 35 per cent of the total refurbishment costs of FF1,000 million). Further work is taking place at the station with an expected completion date of 1998.

The official SNCF handout on the station also identifies one automatic bank dispenser, six clocks, two letterboxes, seven trolley parks, 10 public card telephones and a nursery!

Left: Eurostars have their own dedicated area at Gare du Nord: but this isn't it! Here a Eurostar train can be seen 'slumming' in the main station area, rubbing shoulders with a TGV.

Brussels Midi

Opened in 1846 the original Brussels Midi was called the Gare des Bogards and was situated on the Place Roupe. The next Brussels Midi station — on the site of the existing structure — was opened in 1869: it was a wonderful period piece with a grand victory arch. The existing station — the third — was built in 1949. It is the hub not only of SNCB's Eurostar connection but also the joint venture, Thalys TGV to Paris, and passenger levels of over 200,000 per day through the station complex are anticipated by the end of the century. Thalys runs to Amsterdam (currently on existing lines) and it is anticipated that within two years the other leg to Aachen and Cologne will open. There are plans for DB ICE high-speed trains to start running into Brussels, which in turn will reduce the journey time to a number of destinations.

Midi is undergoing a major renovation and rebuilding programme which started in autumn 1992. The international station is divided into the Eurostar area (platforms 1 and 2) completed in 1994, segregated for Tunnel security, and the Thalys TGV lines (platforms 3 to 6) completed

in 1995. Outside on land purchased by the railway, a major new complex of offices, underground car-park and station improvements is planned to open in 2000 to provide Brussels with a station fit for the third millennium. With 120,000sq m of office space, 10,000sq m of shops, 10,000sq m of leisure facilities and 2,500 parking spaces, it will be a major improvement to the area surrounding the station.

The Eurostar terminal is already constructed to a high specification with a bar and shops as well as the check-in and immigration facilities and escalators to allow ease of passenger movement.

Brussels Midi serves the south of the city with all trains northward stopping at the main station, Brussels Central. Midi is on the Clemenceau to Simonis underground line.

Ashford International

Ashford in Kent has been an important railway town since the middle of the last century when the South Eastern Railway established its locomotive works there in 1847. Although the loco works closed in 1962, the wagon works and emu maintenance depot at Chart Leacon maintained its importance. But it would be Eurostar that saw Ashford blossom once more when it was chosen to be the terminal for passengers arriving by car and for the south-east England catchment area. With excellent access to the M20 and via the M20 to the M25 and the whole of England's motorway system, Ashford is superbly situated with splendid parking facilities in a specially constructed, secure multi-storey car park. It is so much easier for many Eurostar passengers to join the train an hour after it leaves London (at present; with the high-speed link journey times should improve dramatically) than get to Waterloo an hour earlier — the first summer train of the day is timed as an 04.54 Waterloo departure.

The renovation of the existing station and the building of the new international station complex cost £100 million and was a requirement of the Channel Tunnel Act. It was designed by Nick Derbyshire (initially of BR) and built by John Laing, who started work in October 1993. HRH Duke of Kent opened the new domestic station on 6 September 1995; the International station opened for ticket sales on 7 January and for Eurostar services on 8 January 1996. HRH Duke of Kent officially opened the International station on 28 February 1996.

The ground floor of the international station comprises an immigration and arrivals hall, ticket office, left luggage facility and entrance concourse with links to the local station whose train departure timings are displayed on a monitor in a corner of the concourse under the long walkway to the multi-storey car park (designed, it is said, on the ground plan of local Leeds Castle). The upper level consists of check-in, security screening, departure hall for 800 people, regular user lounge with office facilities, bar, café and access to the central island's two Eurostar platforms (3 and 4) which have been extended to accommodate 400m-

Below: The 10.23 Waterloo-Paris service passes through Ashford on 28 November 1995 showing the new Ashford International station. An engineers' train is at platform 4. *BM*

Left: The Eurostar concourse at Ashford International.

Below: All the excitement of the Continent is only a short train ride away for passengers waiting at Ashford International.

long trains. At the time of writing Ashford was served each day by eight outward and five inward Paris trains and four each way to and from Brussels.

The rebuilding of Ashford station also saw the construction of a major signalbox which controls traffic from the Tunnel to Petts Wood. Trains from South Eastern's Ashford station serve the south coast and Kent, with London Bridge, Waterloo East and Charing Cross as their London destinations.

The author has unpleasant memories of Heathrow terminals at six in the morning, prefaced by a very early alarm call in Surrey and unbelievable traffic jams at the entrances to the airport (the only comfort being the knowledge that there were at least 5,000 others in similar discomfort). An admittedly equally early call followed by comparatively traffic-free motoring through the Surrey/Kent countryside resulted recently in arriving in such good time that an espresso could be enjoyed before boarding the 06.15 to Paris. Three hours later in real time, four hours by the clock, I was able to enjoy another coffee in Paris Nord!

Lille-Europe

Lille-Europe is set in the massive Euralille development, which was conceived by Pierre Mauroy, Lille's mayor and a former Prime Minister.

Euralille is based primarily on three structures which straddle the station and together form the 92,000sq m Business Centre. It is a new station built about 400m south of the existing Lille-Flandres which looks after local traffic and is the terminus for the Paris-Lille TGV. Lille-Europe — an international station and a hub of the TGV system — was specially built at a cost of FF252 million to the designs of architect J. M. Duthilleul. It was opened on 6 May 1994 by President Mitterrand; he was joined by a TGV-R which had made an inaugural run from the new No 1 platform at Brussels Midi. On board were Belgian Prime Minister Jean-Luc Dehaene and European Union President Jacques Delors. All three travelled on to Coquelles to join Her Majesty the Queen and the opening festivities.

Lille-Europe is the junction for Eurostar trains to and from London — the routes split at Lille to go south to Paris or east to Brussels. It also connects to the TGV system allowing passengers to get to the following destinations without going through Paris by use of a cutoff to the east of the capital: Lyon, Montpellier, Marseille, Nice, Nantes, Rennes, Quimper, Bordeaux, Dijon, Avignon, Poitiers and Tours. There are six platforms. Euralille is connected to the city by the VAL metro system. It has parking for 1,500 vehicles. The TGV tracks are below ground level to allow the site to be crossed by the Le Corbusier road viaduct.

Lille is also home to the Centre de Contrôle Voyageurs, Lille — the CCV — which is covered in Chapter 3.

Below: The concourse at Lille, a busy hub with connections to the SNCF TGV system.

Gare RER,
Chessy Marne-la-Vallée

The RER station is some 300m from the gates of Eurodisney Paris and equally close to the Eurodisney hotels. Eurostar arrives here 3hr 15min after leaving London with probably the happiest and youngest travellers to be found on an international transport system anywhere in the world. It opened for business on 29 May 1995 and is visited direct by one ex-London trains per day.

The station is well equipped for the local railhead role fringed on one side by the resort's bus station and on the other by the station for RER Line A which travels centrally through Paris (stopping for example at Châtelet, Charles de Gaulle Étoile [Arc de Triomphe] and La Défense).

Left: Celebration time at Eurodisney as LCR are chosen to construct the CTRL.

Calais-Fréthun

On 24 May 1994 Calais-Fréthun opened to the public at a cost of FF27 million. On the TGV Nord Europe line from Paris it is a regional and TGV station: some Eurostar trains stop at Calais allowing embarkation for London or Roissy (Charles de Gaulle).

Right: With the Eurotunnel loading ramps in the background, a Eurostar pulls into Calais-Fréthun.

The Depots

Servicing of Eurostar trains was from the start intended to be international. This culture of servicing other companies' engines has been much stronger on the Continent than in the UK. With Eurostar, every trainset — projected to carry out two inward and two outward journeys each day — would require servicing and a safety examination every night to be undertaken at the most convenient depot. Planned preventive maintenance will be undertaken at nine-day intervals, usually at the trainset's home depot.

North Pole

Named after a local public house near Wormwood Scrubs, North Pole is Eurostar's principal depot. Built at a cost of £80 million, the main building is 3km long but only 70m wide, sandwiched between a public park and the Great Western mainline railway to the West Country of England. It occupies a site once used by five former railway locations: Barlby Rd carriage depot, West London Sidings, Aberdare Sidings, Middle Sidings and Kimberley Sidings and is said to pass through three London boroughs.

Exceptional design allows for the maintenance and cleaning of up to 13 complete Eurostar trains a night. Eurostar trains arrive from Waterloo via the West London line and

Below: Set Nos 3002/3001 at North Pole. *BM*

Above: Nos 3102 and 3018 at North Pole on 12 February 1995. *BM*

enter North Pole via one of four reception sidings running on 750V dc. Beyond these sidings, inside the depot, the power is 25kV ac. (A short section of the overhead wire can be energised at 3,000V dc to enable testing of the trains for services in Belgium.)

The trains run through the washing plant — specially designed not to waste water — before moving to the lavatory discharge area. The toilets are aircraft style and can usually go three days without needing to be discharged; heavier than normal use can make the discharging more frequent. Reversing into one of the six servicing shed tracks (two of which are electrified), normal routine maintenance sees a Eurostar spend about two hours there. Here pantographs, third-rail current collection systems, bogies and brakes are tested while internal cleaning of the crew and passenger areas is carried out simultaneously. The entire facility has been designed with security in mind, and not many enthusiasts get to visit it.

After routine maintenance the train can be pushed back into service or go to the east side of the site (crossing the West London line in the process) for heavier work. London-Paris/ Brussels trains have to split into two to get into the workshop. Two of the roads are now fitted with 25kV overhead, but the remainder require shunting by either a Class 08 shunter or a Scharfenberg coupling-fitted Class 73. The maintenance regime at North Pole is set down by the Comité International de Maintenance Eurostar and is also followed at Le Landy and Forest.

Components for the Eurostar fleet are held at the International Supply Centre (ISC). An interesting European touch is the naming of the five training suites: Stephenson (after George), Walschaerts (after the one-time head of the Belgian Mechelen workshops), Chapelon (French steam design genius), de Glehn (British-born French locomotive designer) and Stanier (after the famous CME of the LMS who designed such locos as the 'Coronation' class Pacifics). The training centre is becoming essential as more and more Eurostars arrive at North Pole. Much of the training is learning French — 7% — because the language of the maintenance depots is French — indeed the

exams and inspections are named in French, for example the Examen Confort, Opération de Confort Esthétique .

The Head of Production Engineering for Eurostar (UK) controls both North Pole and the Manchester International Depot. It and another special facility in Glasgow will see two sets each based there when NoL services begin.

Above: Eurostar outside the service depot at North Pole on 9 December 1993. *BM*

Left: The main building at North Pole — 400m long and 70m wide!

Above: An aerial view of the Eurostar depot at North Pole showing, in the foreground, the reception sidings. Beyond the West London line can be seen the four track repair shed. The smaller building beyond the repair shed is the bogie shop. The Railtrack main line into London Paddington is situated to the north of North Pole depot.

Right: Interior of the repair shed showing the 27 Neuero simultaneous lifting jacks which are capable of lifting a complete TMST half-set. BM

Le Landy and Forest

Unlike Britain, where the creation of EPS as a separate entity within the railway industry was mirrored by the construction of separate maintenance facilities, in both France and Belgium the existing state railways — SNCF and SNCB respectively — were to form each country's participant in the Eurostar consortium. This meant that for both countries it was possible to integrate the TMST maintenance facilities within the overall requirements for the European high-speed network.

The SNCF depot, Le Landy, is situated immediately to the north of Paris Gare du Nord on the western side of the running lines. It handles the maintenance not only of the Eurostar TMST sets but also the TGVs used on the LGV-Nord and the Thalys units. Le Landy is a major complex with three distinct elements. Le Landy Pleyel (the northernmost section) primarily deals with the maintenance of TGV coaches. Le Landy Centre handles Eurostar rakes as well as those units used on Thalys and TGV-Nord services. Finally, Le Landy Sud undertakes routine examinations and the preparation and despatch of stock.

Le Landy originally dates back to 1878 but the site underwent major modification for the introduction of TGV and Eurostar services and now covers some 30 hectares. Le Landy Centre was entirely rebuilt in 1992 for the TGV-Nord and Eurostar services. Its facilities include a three-track 400m-long shed for Eurostar stock. Amongst equipment allocated to Le Landy are 16 Eurostar rakes, 10 rakes of triple-voltage Thalys stock and six rakes of quadruple-voltage Thalys stock.

The SNCB depot is at Forest. This is located to the southwest of Brussels Midi and is also to the western side of the running lines that carry Eurostar services from Lille into Brussels. The original depot on this site was an SNCB EMU depot, but this was closed in October 1990 and its stock transferred elsewhere to allow for conversion to the TMST facility. It is planned that Forest will have the capacity to service five TMST rakes per night. As with Le Landy, Forest is also tasked with handling TGVs used on the Thalys network, with the stock occupying separate sides of a large shed although there is commonality of workforce.

Left: Pictured at Lille Flanders station on 5 October 1995 (during the Eurailspeed 95 exhibition) is TMST Nos 3201/3202 alongside RENFE (Spanish State Railways) AVE (a derivative from the French TGV) No 16. *BM*

The Lines

C urrently the line distances are as
follows:

Waterloo–Ashford 93.5km (58.1 miles)
Ashford–Tunnel portal north 21.2km (13.2 miles)
Tunnel 50.5km (31.4 miles)
Tunnel portal south–Calais-Fréthun 3.4km (2.1 miles)
Calais-Fréthun–Lille 101km (62.6 miles)
Lille–Paris 225km (140 miles)
Total Waterloo–Paris: 495km (307.4 miles)

Waterloo–Lille 269km (167.4 miles)
Lille–Brussels 106km (66 miles)
Total: Waterloo–Brussels: 376km (233.4 miles)

Below: The 12.31 Brussels-Waterloo service passes Dollands Moor Yard on 23 February 1995. Class 92 Nos 92021 and 92022 stand in the yard. *Peter W. Howard*

Infrastructure

Left: The scenery isn't always as good as the ride: a European industrial landscape.

Below: The infrastructure of the London section of the journey isn't always conducive to high speed running!
BM

Power Supply

One of the biggest technical achievements of the Eurostar trains is the ability to cope with the different power supplies available in each country. Because railways developed pretty much independently of each other and because of the conditions that existed in those countries, Europe has ended up with an amorphous, unintegrated railway system with huge differences at almost every operating level. It is only in happier post-World War 2 times that international co-operation has led to through-running to a large degree and resulted in these problems being addressed and remedied.

The Eurostar trains have to cope with three different power supply voltages: 750V dc with power collection by means of retractable shoegear from the third-rail on the southern part of the UK rail system (mainly designed and built for commuter traffic from the early years of this century onwards); 25,000V ac collected from overhead catenary in the tunnel, on the new high-speed lines in France and Belgium, lines north of London and, when built, on the British high-speed link; and 3,000V dc from overhead catenary on the conventional Belgian network.

The complexity of this operation was the cause of many of Eurostar's early headaches, particularly from arcing at third-rail gaps. Today those problems are no more. The changeover from one power supply to another system takes place on the move, either by lifting or retracting the pantographs and with neutral sections between the different sources. Each neutral section is about 15m in length.

Below: A good view of the overhead catenary on the French side of the tunnel. No 3215 has one of its pantographs raised to collect current.

France

France has led the way in the construction of lines for high-speed running. And it was the French who ensured that the Three Capitals service would be run at high speed when it announced that the Calais-Paris line would be a TGV high-speed line. The phenomenal success of the French TGV, running at 300km/hr, did not happen overnight. On 27 September 1981 the first length of line worked by TGVs — the southern section of the Paris Sud-Est line — opened for public service. It heralded the start of a nationwide system of new high-speed track enabling journey times throughout France to be slashed. Building these lines proved less problematic than building lines for the steam railways of the past had been: the incredible power of electric traction meant that gradients of 3.5 per cent could be handled, and the comfortable ride given by new low-slung rolling stock meant that the passengers could survive the ride!

Along with the improved train equipment, signalling, catenary and power supply, the new system had to be grafted onto the existing SNCF system: it was just too expensive to consider building completely new line into the major cities and through certain tunnels and other barriers. Upgrading the old lines was therefore essential and was duly accomplished successfully. Today TGVs travel to numerous destinations on new as well as conventional track.

The French are also much more pragmatic when it comes to permissions for new track. Both the British and Belgians have been bogged down in the politics of where the track will go — unsurprising when you consider the relative sizes and population density of the countries involved: France is four times the size of England but has virtually the same population. The French 'Declaration of Public Utility' confers wide powers including compulsory land purchase: while this does not mean that the French system is more draconian or less fair than the others, the consultation period is always much shorter!

The TGV Nord Europe line was the third TGV track to be built — it would have preceded the TGV Atlantique (the Brittany arm from Paris Montparnasse to Le Mans [for Rennes] opened on 24 September 1989; the Aquitaine arm to Tours opened on 30 September 1990; TGV services use existing lines beyond Tours) had the Channel Tunnel project got off the ground sooner.

The track opened in two stages: from Paris to Arras on 23 May 1993; Arras to Lille and Calais in September 1993. Services on Eurostar

Below: France has led the way in the construction of high speed line for Eurostar.

started using the line for passenger services on 14 November 1994. The high-speed line starts just outside Paris Nord and runs for 333km (207 miles), splitting at Frétin to run to Lille and the Tunnel on the one hand and the Belgian border which is only 15.7km (9.8 miles) away on the other. The line runs next to the A1 for more than 130km. To complicate matters, environmental work had to be done to preserve the Forêt de l'Épinoy and de Guines by replanting trees at their edges.

The line needed an impressive amount of infrastructure: 329 bridges, 161 'ouvrages hydrauliques' (culverts) and 10 viaducts with a total length of 5,600m, whilst 32km of walls and 41km of banking was used to reduce noise pollution in sensitive areas. 1,350km of rail was laid on 1,125 million 'traverses' (sleepers). Three million tonnes of ballast were used to stabilise the line. All this allows the Eurostar to travel safely and comfortably at 300km/hr with plans to increase to 350.

The Roissy/Charles de Gaulle airport TGV station (situated on the route to Eurodisney) opened at the end of 1995. The track layout is similar to Lille's, but the through Eurostar tracks are not encased. Through- running is limited to 230km/hr. Charles de Gaulle will be less than three hours away from Waterloo once everything is open; this in itself could well stimulate business.

England

The difference between the French track and that of Belgium and England is nowhere better exemplified than the deadpan delivery of one of SNCF's Eurostar leaflets: the train, it says, leaves the tunnel for the countryside of Kent at 120km/hr. Each morning between 07.00 and 10.00 it must join 150 commuter trains and each evening between 16.00 and 19.00, 132 commuter trains, to make its way to London. It is hardly surprising therefore that journey times will stay around three hours (the record is actually 2hr 37min) until the new high-speed link is opened.

The British route from Waterloo to the Tunnel had to slog its way along some of the most busy tracks in the world as commuters head to and from London. If you miss your pathway, Eurostar's supertrain is condemned to

Below: Eurostar passing through a wintry French landscape.

follow a regional train until a passing can be arranged. On top of this, the sheer size of the London conurbation and the restrictions on running speed which apply through residential areas, make for a slow journey in comparison with speeds attained in France.

This is not to say that the ride is poor. Far from it: apart from the excellent scenery there were some line improvements undertaken by BR before privatisation and Railtrack following its takeover of track control. The track improvements cost £300 million and involved rebuilding 104 bridges — particularly 94 on the freight routes to increase clearances for containers and 10 in the London area — increasing power supplies and installing passing loops. The main works were:

- Upgrading the two boat train routes — now rechristened Channel Tunnel Routes (CTRs) — (CTR1 runs London-Bickley Jn-Sevenoaks-Tonbridge-Ashford and CTR2 Swanley-Maidstone East-Ashford with a length of 66km [41 miles]) including bringing forward the Network SouthEast domestic scheme to Chiselhurst-Folkestone, leaving the signalling in the hands of a new IECC (integrated electronic control centre) signalbox at Ashford, strengthening third-rail power supply and gauge clearance work
- Electrification to 750V dc third-rail system of the 33.8km (21 miles) of track between Tonbridge and Redhill for freight
- Upgrading, resignalling and equipment with Southern third-rail power supply of

the 11km (7 mile) long West London line between the boat train routes and Willesden through Kensington Olympia. All this cost £40 million including strengthening work to Chelsea Bridge and re-laying cwr track to fulfil Channel Tunnel Act commitment to noise controls over the whole lines

- Construction of the Stewarts Lane chord between Queenstown Road junction and Linford Street junction to enable Tunnel traffic access to Waterloo arriving on the boat train routes from Victoria. This two-track viaduct, with a box-like structure over the approach lines to Waterloo, is long enough to hold Eurostar services should traffic from Victoria be using the lines. The viaduct has more than 40 spans and is about 1km (0.6 mile) long.
- Reinstating the line providing access to the West London Line from Waterloo. This is the Sheepcote Chord and is mainly used by stock moving to and from North Pole
- Re-laying 27km (17 miles) of line around Ashford up to Continental Jn where tracks to the Tunnel diverge with those to Dollands Moor.

The new CTRL from St Pancras to the Tunnel, however, will improve the situation substantially. It will be one of the largest infrastructure projects in the UK over the latter part of the 1990s and is programmed to open in 2003. It is detailed in Chapter 6.

Belgium

As in England, the Belgian high-speed line is yet to be completed (see Chapter 6). Currently the Eurostars follow the old SNCB line 94 via Tournai and Ath.

Below: A Eurostar approaches Vauxhall with the 08.23 Waterloo-Paris on 9 September 1995. *Chris Wilson*

The Trains

O n 31 December 1989, a contract was signed between British Rail, SNCF and SNCB for the purchase of 31 Eurostar trains — this was subsequently increased to 34 'sets', as the full complement of two engines and 18 carriages is termed. A consortium of train manufacturers was formed to deliver the order. This was called the TransManche Super Train Group (TMSTG) with GEC-Alsthom taking the lead. The latter is a joint venture between GEC and Alsthom of France (the designers and builders of SNCF's TGV trains) on which Eurostar is based. The power cars are built at the Belfort works in France and moved to Birmingham for mating with the coaches.

In total, with regional Eurostars, 38 sets have been built, shared between the three railways. European Passenger Services own 18 sets (11 Three Capitals trains and seven regional ones), SNCF 16 sets and SNCB four sets. This ownership is invisible to the travelling public — the trains all have identical liveries, the crew wear the same uniforms — but it is a bookkeeping requirement. Furthermore they all receive heavy overhauls in the home ownership depot.

A technical description of the Eurostar trains is given in Appendix 2.

Below: Formed of Class 373 units Nos 3229/30, the 12.53 Waterloo-Paris Eurostar winds away from Ashford International on Bastille Day 1996, after its scheduled stop. *BM*

DID YOU KNOW ?

- The trains are about 800 tons in weight and carry around 800 passengers.
- They are about 400m (1,312ft) long — taller in length than the Eiffel Tower — and travel at up to 300kph (186mh).
- They have 12 electric motors (four per power car and two per power carriage) that together equal the power of 20 Formula 1 cars, developing 12,200kW tractive power.
- Eurostar takes 3,500m (11,483ft) to stop from a speed of 300kph — a distance equivalent to eight times its own length. In an emergency stop the train absorbs 2.8 million joules of energy — enough to boil 8,000litres (14,078pints) of water or run a domestic electric fire nonstop for two weeks.
- Eurostar has an equivalent number of seats as two Boeing 747 aircraft — 794 passengers (210 in First Class, 584 in Second) in 18 coaches.

- The train is as long as 47 London double decker buses placed end to end.
- When laden the train is as heavy as 20 articulated lorries.
- The maximum power dissipated by the rheostatic braking unit could supply over 600 average domestic properties.
- The full braking force is equivalent to the thrust of two of the most powerful modern aircraft jet engines.
- Each of the 12 electric traction motors has the equivalent power of over 800 washing machine motors.
- Currently the Eurostar fleet covers a distance comparable to 200 times around the world in one year.
- The cost of each Eurostar is £23 million.
- A TGV running at 300kph for 100km (62 miles) only consumes 2.2 litres of fuel per passenger: a car running at 120kph has an energy consumption of 8.8litres for two passengers.

Above: The 12.14 Waterloo-Brussels Eurostar passes newly-erected sound reflecting fencing at Shortlands on 14 January 1996. *BM*

Into Service

From its conception Eurostar has been a unique partnership between three separate railways resulting in a truly European train. Every part of it is designed seamlessly to allow tri-national operation in such a way that the passenger cannot tell to which railway the train belongs or indeed in which country it is running. The train crews are bi- or multilingual and wear the same uniforms; all the drivers are cleared to run through the full journey (except that at Kensington Olympia, North of London, drivers will take over from international drivers and vice versa); maintenance is performed at whichever depot is most conveniently located. Above all, the same high standard of service is delivered whatever your destination.

Drivers and Crew

In 1991 one of the first things EPS had to do, as did its SNCF and SNCB partners, was to find drivers capable of through-running on Three Capitals services. The training was based at Holmes House, next door to Waterloo and now opposite the Esprit offices. As well as the essential language training, Holmes House is home to the Eurostar simulator upon which new drivers learn the ropes and old hands have their annual assessments and checks.

The company had to show the two Continental systems that British drivers were capable of all the duties that would be asked of them — driving high-speed trains in an environment very different to that which exists in Britain; that they could cope with the language barriers (something for which Britons

are not particularly well known!); and that the training systems could ensure a high calibre of train crew. In turn EPS also had to satisfy itself that the SNCF and SNCB crews could cope with the intense traffic regime which exists in southern England; after all it would be some years before the CTRL was established.

The first thing EPS did was select the

Left: With extensive engineering work taking place east of Ashford, a Eurostar passes by forming the 10.27 from Waterloo to Brussels on 28 November 1995. *BM*

Above: Passengers preparing to board a Eurostar service in the new terminal at Waterloo International. The on-board crew are there, air hostess-style to welcome and help you on board.

personnel. It advertised within BR for professionals with a minimum of five years' main line competence, clean disciplinary records and — initially — for people who had driven long-distance high-speed services — HSTs or electric locos on WCML or ECML. In fact, experience has shown that proficient shorter-run drivers of suburban trains actually make excellent drivers of Eurostars: it's about attitude and aptitude.

After an initial interview and medical tests the candidates went for an intensive three-week language course before being taken to Lille for a week where they lived *en famille* and worked with the French. After a final assessment to ensure they could handle Continental driving (tests on signalling etc) EPS had its drivers. It had been a tough selection course and only one in five of the initial candidates passed.

The thing that became immediately apparent was just how well the British railwaymen and 'Les Cheminots' got on together. Friendships established in those early days have stood the test of time and make working for EPS very enjoyable.

What are the most noticeable differences between Britain and the Continent? To begin

with EPS was amazed at the quality and quantity of the men, machines and infrastructure. It was used to BR which had been in the doldrums for some years and which already had to cope with a reduced level of real spending, with cost cutting and 'overhead trimming' to such an extent that working in France was like going into a sweet shop. Their tracks all seemed to be two or three roads wider than ours; trains used to pass depots full of rolling stock and locos. Today things may be changing but it is noticeable that the SNCF and SNCB systems are much more modern and better appointed than that in Britain. What's more, their machinery is all home-grown. How many railway manufacturing companies are there left in this country?

This difference in traffic was summed up well by a French driver travelling through southern England for the first time: 'How do you run such a thick system on such a thin infrastructure?' The French and Belgians have their own intensive traffic areas but were amazed at the antiquity of BR's machinery and the sheer amount of traffic.

The other big difference was in the way that British drivers learnt their routes. On the

Continent there's much more dependence on the 'book'. In Britain drivers learn their route and familiarise themselves with it thoroughly, reducing the need for book dependence. Interestingly, both sets of drivers have learnt from each other and on Eurostar the drivers go for the best of all worlds with a strong familiarity with the route.

Driver management and monitoring is an important part of high-speed services. It's important that drivers work closely to their parameters and that they perform their duties efficiently. To monitor this, on top of the usual range of checks each country places on its own system, the Eurostar trains are equipped with 'black boxes'. Downloaded they provide a record of each and every train movement and system, allowing drivers' performances to be monitored carefully. As might be expected after the intensive training, Eurostar drivers are top operators and there are few problems. On BR, driving standards managers go out with each driver every two years or so; on Eurostar the international drivers are checked every six months.

Eurostar is known for its speed and the operator monitors it very carefully: regular running at more than 2km/hr above the speed limit causes concern. At 6km/hr the train systems start to complain and above that the automatic brakes come on and the driver has a lot to answer for. Wouldn't it be interesting if car drivers had such strict monitoring of their performance!

Each year drivers have to take a set of proficiency exams — oral, computer-based and simulator-based — for all three national systems and the Tunnel. Eurostar drivers' performance has been exemplary and the selection system has stood the test of time — the loyalty and ability of the drivers are shown by a simple statistic: all the recruited drivers are still with Eurostar (UK) Ltd.

Eurostar (UK) Ltd has currently in Britain approx 130 drivers for international and regional services including a number of Train Managers trained to manoeuvre the train in the Channel Tunnel in the event of an emergency.

This shows another difference between Eurostar and normal British train operations, for

Below: Passengers prepare to board the early morning Eurostar from London Waterloo to Paris as it arrives at Ashford International. *Colin Boocock*

example the position of Train Manager, who works closely with the driver to ensure safety and comfort for the passengers, like the 4Cs catering staff, is multilingual.

Indeed, for most positions a level of foreign languages must be achieved. For drivers and traction inspectors this meant a minimum acceptable level of competence had to be assessed and reached. This was done by means of a series of tests and exams — including a full simulator run with conversations with French and Belgian regulators and railwaymen — at the end of which a certificate shows that the holder is '[a] Proficient user of French in a railway environment'.

The training programme was called *En Train de Parler* and was put together by the universities of North and South London in conjunction with EPS language specialists. It's a very proud moment when the certificate is presented.

The Centre de Contrôle Voyageurs, Lille

Housed 'round the back' of Lille - Flandres, the CCV's main function is to act as the day-to-day operations centre and to co-ordinate the disposition of Eurostar trains around the service requirements. It sits alongside Railfreight Distribution and is in contact with drivers, signalboxes and operators to ensure smooth running. The CCV must ensure sufficient stock at each location to perform the required timetable duties, with the intention of reducing the amount of unremunerative running to a minimum. On top of this, if anything goes wrong, it can be very helpful to a driver to be able to discuss problems with a fellow countryman.

Right: The 10.23 Waterloo International-Paris Gare du Nord service nears Ashford International on a wintry 27 January 1996, formed of TMST Nos 3015 (leading) and 3016. *BM*

Catering

The need for on-board catering is obvious: as is the benefit of having a captive market for over three hours. On-board catering is the charge of 4Cs — the Cross-Channel Catering Company. Originally part of Sabena and now part of Swissair, 4Cs has three satellites which handle the day-to-day operations: in Paris Nordrail, in Brussels Restorail and in the UK Rail Gourmet UK Ltd.

Food on board Eurostar consists of airline style main meals (free and served to your seat in First Class; available from the bar in Standard) and a trolley service which takes hot and cold drinks through the Standard Class section of the train. Because of the hygiene requirements and the pre-preparation, there is a strong commercial need to judge accurately how many customers there will be. Working closely with Eurostar, Rail Gourmet, which has secure offices in the bowels of Waterloo, makes its first forecast of food requirements about a week before departure: it will continue to plan in detail down to as little as five minutes before the journey. The ease of access to the platforms from below, makes such fine-tuning as this possible.

Left: Airline-style meals are provided for passengers travelling First Class.

menu

Bon Appétit

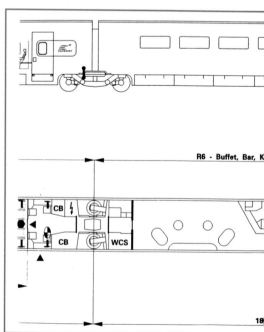

R6 - Buffet, Bar, K

CB

CB   WCS

Above and far right: A typical menu for passengers travelling in Premium First, offered in three languages.

Right: Arrangement of catering vehicles.

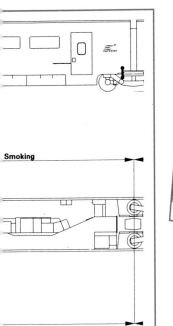

Smoking

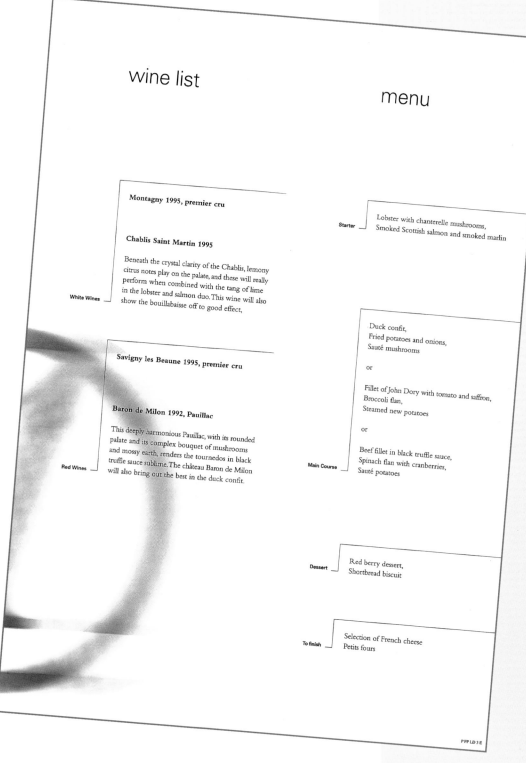

wine list

menu

White Wines

Montagny 1995, premier cru

Chablis Saint Martin 1995

Beneath the crystal clarity of the Chablis, lemony citrus notes play on the palate, and these will really perform when combined with the tang of lime in the lobster and salmon duo. This wine will also show the bouillabaisse off to good effect.

Red Wines

Savigny les Beaune 1995, premier cru

Baron de Milon 1992, Pauillac

This deeply harmonious Pauillac, with its rounded palate and its complex bouquet of mushrooms and mossy earth, renders the tournedos in black truffle sauce sublime. The château Baron de Milon will also bring out the best in the duck confit.

Starter
Lobster with chanterelle mushrooms,
Smoked Scottish salmon and smoked marlin

Main Course
Duck confit,
Fried potatoes and onions,
Sauté mushrooms

or

Fillet of John Dory with tomato and saffron,
Broccoli flan,
Steamed new potatoes

or

Beef fillet in black truffle sauce,
Spinach flan with cranberries,
Sauté potatoes

Dessert
Red berry dessert,
Shortbread biscuit

To finish
Selection of French cheese
Petits fours

PFP LD 3 E

Above left: The buffet/bar provides a full catering serivice.

71

Euro Despatch Centre/ Esprit Europe

Eurostar, in common with the airlines, has only limited space on board and cannot accommodate huge amounts of luggage. There are holds on the trains and, with the frequency of service, it is certainly possible to take bulky packages.

Attached to this service is Esprit, making use of Eurostar's speed and frequency to provide an express documents service.

Eurostar Services

PASSENGERS

There was a gradual build-up of Eurostar services: On 14 November 1994 the Discovery service was launched. This began with eight trains (two a day in both directions between London and Paris and Brussels). On 23 January 1995 the service frequency increased substantially and it is intended in the future to have one train an hour in each direction.

The traffic in 1996 built up substantially — over 50 per cent of the rail-plus-air travellers between the three capitals. The service has continued to expand and despite the initial and well-documented problems, today Eurostar achieves high standards of reliability, comparing favourably with air travel on the same routes. Currently, the autumn 1996 timetable identifies the following services (on top of this London-Eurodisney services have been instituted. During August 1997 these ran at 19.23 from London — arriving Eurodisney, Paris 13.44; and 18.35 from Eurodisney back to England — arriving at 20.39).

As an example of this in operation, the figures on the right are the CCV figures for Saturday 3 August 1996 showing arrival at, and departure from, the Tunnel's portals.

One thing that has certainly improved under LCR is the marketing of the Eurostar product. With widespread confusion between the operations of Eurostar and Eurotunnel and, initially, a stylish if impenetrable sales campaign, the marketing strategy needed improvement. The popular advertising using TV's *Eurotrash* star Antoines de Caunes is certainly more obvious.

Expansion of advertising from the south-east catchment area is planned — but with Ashford's substantial capacity still under-utilised, the south-east still needs enticing to use Eurostar. The establishment of the interconnection, allowing TGVs from Lille direct access to LGV without changing in Paris, opens up a substantial number of destinations; the opening of NoL services in Britain should similarly boost traffic with the increased accessibility.

Passenger Traffic*:

Portal South to North

No	Passing Time South	Passing Time North	Service
9007	08.39	09.00	Paris-London
9113	09.12	09.33	Brussels-London
9011	09.37	09.58	Paris-London
9117	10.07	10.28	Brussels-London
9015	10.39	11.00	Paris-London
9019	11.42	12.03	Paris-London
9125	12.12	12.33	Brussels-London
9025	13.12	13.33	Paris-London
9133	14.12	14.33	Brussels-London
9031	14.34	14.55	Paris-London
9039	16.42	17.03	Paris-London
9145	17.09	17.30	Brussels-London
9043	17.37	17.58	Paris-London
9047	18.34	18.58	Paris-London
9153	19.04	19.25	Brussels-London
9051	19.42	20.03	Paris-London
9053	20.04	19.25	Eurodisney-London
9157	20.07	20.30	Brussels-London
9059	21.37	21.58	Paris-London

Portal North to South

No	Passing Time North	Passing Time South	Service
9002	08.33	08.54	London-Paris
9110	09.08	09.29	London-Brussels
9006	09.38	09.59	London-Paris
9010	10.38	10.59	London-Paris
9116	10.41	11.02	London-Brussels
9012	11.03	11.24	London-Paris
9014	11.38	11.59	London-Eurodisney
9018	12.33	12.54	London-Paris
9124	12.36	12.57	London-Brussels
9024	14.06	14.27	London-Paris
9132	14.41	15.02	London-Brussels
9028	15.08	15.29	London-Paris
9140	16.33	16.54	London-Brussels
9038	17.33	17.54	London-Paris
9042	18.38	18.59	London-Paris
9152	19.37	19.58	London-Brussels
9048	20.03	20.24	London-Paris
9156	20.41	21.02	London-Brussels
9052	21.08	21.29	London-Paris

*Data correct at time of compilation.

Eurostar

Right: The Eurostar timetable for the period 30 June to 27 September 1997.

Far right: The 16.13 Paris-Waterloo approaching Westenhanger on 4 April 1996.
Michael J. Collins

Monday to Saturday — 30 June to 27 September 1997

London ▲ Paris

	②	③																		
Waterloo Int.	05.08	06.19	07.23	07.53	08.23	08.53	09.53	10.23	11.57	12.53	13.57	15.23	15.53	16.23	17.15	17.48	17.57	18.53	19.23	19.53
Ashford Int.	06.16	07.19	08.24		09.23		10.53				13.53				17.24				19.54	20.23
Calais-Fréthun	08.55								14.29						17.56				20.26	20.29
Lille Europe						11.50										19.26				
Paris Nord	09.23	10.23	11.23	11.47	12.23	12.53	13.53	14.17	15.56	16.53	17.56	19.23	19.53	20.29	21.17	21.53	21.56	22.53	23.23	23.47
Train number	9078	9002	9006	9008	9010	9012	9016	9018	9024	9028	9032	9038	9040	9042	9046	9048	9052	9054	9056	
First Class Meals	B	B	B	B	B	B	B	L	L	L	LM	LM	LM	D	D	D	D	D	D	

Paris ▲ London

	②	③						②	②							②				
Paris Nord	06.37	06.37	07.16	08.13	09.10	09.43	10.19	11.43	12.19	13.04	14.16	14.49	15.19	16.07	17.10	18.19	19.19	20.07	20.49	21.13
Lille Europe						10.11				12.44									21.09	
Calais-Fréthun	08.04	08.04							14.31				17.34							
Ashford Int.				09.11			10.41				14.08				17.11	18.11		20.14	21.11	22.11
Waterloo Int.	08.46	08.39	09.09	10.13	11.09	11.43	12.13	13.43	14.13	15.09	16.09	16.43	17.13	18.13	19.13	20.13	21.13	22.13	22.43	23.16
Train number	9005	9005	9007	9011	9015	9017	9019	9025	9027	9031	9035	9037	9039	9043	9047	9051	9055	9059	9061	9063
First Class Meals	B	B	B	L	LM	LM	L	L	L	L	LM	LM	L	D	D	D	D	D	D	D

London ▲ Brussels

	②								②	③	④
Waterloo Int.	06.53	08.27	09.27	10.27	12.27	14.23	17.19	17.23	18.27	19.52	09.23
Ashford Int.	07.53	09.27	10.27		13.27			18.23	19.27	20.40	10.23
Lille Europe	09.56	11.29		13.24	15.29	17.21			21.31		13.28
Brussels	11.10	12.44	13.44	14.38	16.44	18.34	21.38	21.38	22.45	22.09	9014
Train number	9110	9116	9120	9124	9132	9140	9152	9152	9156	9161 9163	
First Class Meals	B	B	LM	L	LM	LM	D	D	D	D D	B

Brussels ▲ London

	②						②	③	④
Brussels	07.31	08.27	10.31	12.31	15.28	17.22	18.27	19.27	18.35
Lille Europe	08.45	09.40	11.45	13.44	16.42	18.36	19.40	20.40	18.37
Ashford Int.	09.41				16.41	18.37	19.42	20.41	21.07	20.39
Waterloo Int.	09.39	10.43	12.43	14.43	17.43	19.39	20.43	21.43	22.09	9063
Train number	9113	9117	9125	9133	9145	9153	9157	9161 9163	
First Class Meals	B	B	L	LM	D	D	D	D D	LD

London ▲ Disneyland® Paris

	④
Waterloo Int.	09.23
Ashford Int.	10.23
Disneyland Paris	13.28
Train number	9014
Meal in Castle Service	B

Disneyland® Paris ▲ London

	④
Disneyland Paris	18.35
Ashford Int.	18.37
Waterloo Int.	20.39
Train number	9063
Meal in Castle Service	LD

Meals
B Breakfast
LM Light Meal
L Lunch
D Dinner
LD Light Dinner

Key
① Fridays only
② Not on Saturdays
③ Saturdays only
④ Daily Service. Complimentary cold meal served in Castle Service

Sunday — 30 June to 27 September 1997

London ▲ Paris

Waterloo Int.	07.10	08.10	08.53	09.53	10.10	11.57	12.53	13.57	15.10	15.53	16.23	17.23	17.57	18.23	18.53	19.23	19.53
Ashford Int.	08.24	09.23			10.53			13.53			17.24			19.23	20.23
Calais-Fréthun										14.29					20.29
Lille Europe			11.50											19.26
Paris Nord	11.23	12.23	12.53	13.53	14.17	15.56	16.53	17.56	19.23	19.53	20.29	21.17	21.56	22.23	22.47	23.23	23.47
Train number	9006	9010	9012	9016	9018	9024	9028	9032	9038	9040	9042	9048	9050	9052	9054	9056	
First Class Meals	B	B	B	L	L	L	LM	LM	LM	D	D	D	D	D	D	D	

Paris ▲ London

Paris Nord	08.07	09.10	09.43	10.19	11.43	12.19	13.04	14.16	14.49	15.19	16.07	17.10	18.19	19.19	20.07	20.49	21.13
Lille Europe			10.11			12.44										21.09
Calais-Fréthun	09.34						14.31				17.34				
Ashford Int.	09.11			10.41				14.08				17.11	18.11		20.14	21.11	22.11
Waterloo Int.	10.30	11.26	11.43	12.30	13.47	14.30	15.26	16.09	16.43	17.13	18.13	19.13	20.13	21.13	22.13	22.43	23.16
Train number	9011	9015	9017	9019	9025	9027	9031	9035	9037	9039	9043	9047	9051	9055	9059	9061	9063
First Class Meals	B	L	LM	L	L	L	L	LM	LM	L	D	D	D	D	D	D	D

London ▲ Brussels

								④
Waterloo Int.	08.14	10.14	12.14	14.10	17.27	18.27	19.27	09.10
Ashford Int.	09.27		13.27			19.27	20.27	10.23
Lille Europe	11.29	13.24	15.29	17.21		21.31		13.28
Brussels	12.44	14.38	16.44	18.34	21.38	22.45	23.43	9014
Train number	9116	9124	9132	9140	9152	9156	9160	B
First Class Meals	B	LM	LM	LM	D	D	D	

Brussels ▲ London

							④
Brussels	08.27	10.31	12.31	15.28	17.22	18.27	19.52	18.35
Lille Europe	09.40	11.45	13.44	16.42	18.36	19.40	19.37
Ashford Int.	09.41			16.41	18.37	19.42	21.07	20.39
Waterloo Int.	10.47	12.47	14.47	17.43	19.39	20.43	22.10	9063
Train number	9117	9125	9133	9145	9157	9163	LD
First Class Meals	B	L	LM	D	D	D	D

London ▲ Disneyland® Paris

	④
London Waterloo Int.	09.10
Ashford Int.	10.23
Disneyland Paris	13.28
Train number	9014
Meal in Castle Service	B

Disneyland® Paris ▲ London

	④
Disneyland Paris	18.35
Ashford Int.	19.37
London Waterloo Int.	20.39
Train number	9063
Meal in Castle Service	LD

Trains on Sundays and Bank Holidays are subject to change.
Please enquire for further details.
Timetable is correct at time of going to press.

FREIGHT

Freight under Railfreight Distribution, which is not part of LCR but which is an important fellow user of the Channel Tunnel, has performed very effectively, nearing its planned level of 35 trains each way. 70 per cent of the traffic is intermodal, 20 per cent automotive. As an example of the services available, the freight traffic on Thursday 8 August 1996 was as follows:

Portal South to North

Passing Time South	Passing Time North	Service
00.38	01.10	Woippy/Somain-Wembley
02.19	02.51	Valenton/Noisy-Wembley
02.27	03.30	Duisberg/Muizen-Wembley
02.36	03.39	Calais-Corby
03.34	04.06	Silla-Dagenham
04.57	06.00	HLP/Light Engine for 4244
06.12	07.15	HLP/Light Engine after 4264
07.30	08.02	HLP/Light Engine after 4404
12.45	13.17	Somain-Wembley
16.50	17.17	Perpignan-Wembley
18.50	19.17	Milan Melzo-Wembley
19.15	19.47	Aluno-Longbridge
20.20	20.47	Novara-Wembley
20.50	21.17	HLP/Light Engine in place of 4269
21.20	21.47	Rogoredo ACI -Wembley
21.45	22.17	HLP/Light Engine in place of 4127
22.20	22.47	HLP/Light Engine in place of 4239
22.50	23.17	Rogoredo CTL -Wembley
23.15	22.47	Riom-Wembley

Below: The 16.27 Waterloo-Brussels Eurostar approaches the entrance to the Channel Tunnel on 3 August 1995. To the right is the 'le Shuttle' complex. *BM*

Portal North to South

Passing Time North	Passing Time South	Service
00.16	00.48	Wembley-Noisy/Valenton
00.22	00.54	Wembley-Muizen/Duisberg
01.37	02.09	Dagenham-Silla
02.52	03.24	HLP/Light Engine in place of 4128
03.50	04.22	Wembley-Perpignan
05.05	05.37	Longbridge-Aluno
05.13	05.45	Wembley-Milan Melzo
05.31	06.03	Wembley-Lille
06.29	07.01	Wembley-Rogoredo ACI
06.44	07.16	Wembley-Rogoredo CTL
07.34	08.06	Wembley-Novara
14.14	14.46	Washwood Heath-Lille
15.44	16.16	Wembley-Lille
18.14	18.46	HLP/Light Engine after 4297
19.44	20.16	HLP/Light Engine for 4273
20.14	20.46	HLP/Light Engine after 4249
21.44	22.16	HLP/Light Engine for 4433
22.14	22.46	HLP/Light Engine after 4247
23.44	00.16	London-Paris

Below: The Class 92 electric locomotives were largely designed for international freight services. Here No 92020 is seen on display at waterloo International — not a regular haunt of these locomotives. Although freight is handled by a separate company, there is a common interest with Eurostar (UK) in the effective use of the Chaanel Tunnel. Eurostar is allocated a number of Class 92s. *Jeremy de Souza*

Timings

Because of the lack of high-speed links in both Britain and Belgium, the timings of the trains are still much slower than the times to come. Nevertheless, the journey times are a quantum leap ahead of the old rail-ferry-rail journey. The logs that follow give a representative cross-section of times, starting with the inaugural run from London to Paris on Monday 14 November 1994 kindly supplied by Alex Obradovic.

Below: Eurostar offers a carrier service between the three capitals and beyond.

Dist	Location	Scheduled (mph)	Actual	Av Speeds
0000	Waterloo	0000 (08.23BST)	0000 (08.22.5)	
01.36	Vauxhall		03.24	
04.23	Brixton		07.59	
			SIGS	
11.94	Bromley South		20.53	
			SIGS	
15.94	Orpington	23.00	28.33	67.6
24.24	Sevenoaks	30.50	35.55	74.8
31.66	Tonbridge	37.00	41.52	67.4
36.94	Paddock Wood	42.00	46.34	
			SIGS	66.7
41.52	Marden		50.41	
43.99	Staplehurst		55.04	
47.38	Headcorn		59.23	76.7
58.24	Ashford	59.00	67.53	
67.58			74.44	81.8
69.14	Continental Jn Channel Tunnel	68.00	75.27	88.9
71.48	UK Portal	70.00	77.22	
102.86	French Portal	91.00	96.29	98.5
104.91	Fréthun	92.00	97.49	154.1
167.6	Lille-Europe	119	122.14	114.3
174.87	Frétin	122.5	126.03	176.1
228.93	Haute Picardie	143	144.28	175.1
297.79	Gonesse Jn	171	168.04	
307.6	Paris Nord	180 (12.24CET)	177.17 (12.20)	

Average speed Waterloo-Paris: 104.1mph
Waterloo-UK Portal: 55.4mph
French Portal-Paris: 152mph

Right: Eurostar rake UK9 (Nos 3016 and 3015) approaches Kensington Olympia with an ecs working from North Pole depot to Waterloo International on 13 January 1995. This set was rostered to work the 15.53 service to Paris. *Chris Wilson*

Right: Ancient and modern at Lambeth on 4 February 1995. The 09.32 'Solent and Sarum' steam special from Waterloo commences its journey and is passed by the 07.31 Eurostar from Brussels Midi to Waterloo International. Completing the picture, a Class 455/9 EMU forms a Waterloo-Shepperton local service. *BM*

Above: The last Eurostar of the day from Waterloo International was, at this date, timed to depart from Paris Nord at 18.53. Formed of Eurostar set Nos 3007 and 3008, the train catches the last rays of the setting sun near Westenhanger on 15 June 1996. *BM*

Left: The 15.23 Waterloo International-Paris Gare du Nord Eurostar service approaches Tonbridge on 30 July 1996, formed of Eurostar set Nos 3224 at the front and 3223 bringing up the rear. *BM*

Chapter 4

A Day in the Life

Eurostar

It is about 07.30; the first passengers are beginning to arrive for the departures for Paris (at 08.23) and Brussels (at 08.27). The ticket offices are open for the sale of tickets to last minute travellers. Eurostar tickets are computer-generated and include details of seat reservations and coach numbers; generally speaking, passenger check-in is straightforward with the intending passengers inserting the tickets into machines that will automatically register each passenger and, once registered, will allow them access to the departures area. Once through the automatic gates, the passenger undergoes a security check before entering the long departure lounge that is situated under the five platforms that form the International station. The lounge offers the passenger a wide range of facilities — shops, cafes, lavatories, information, etc — that make the short wait before boarding pass quickly.

Whilst intending passengers are instructed to arrive no later than 20 minutes prior to departure, there is no such luxury for the train

84

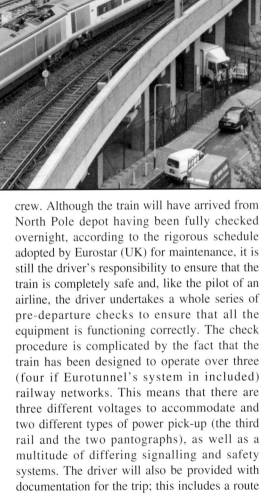

Left: The last
Eurostar of the day,
the 18.53 to Paris
Nord, departing
from Waterloo on
22 May 1996. *BM*

crew. Although the train will have arrived from North Pole depot having been fully checked overnight, according to the rigorous schedule adopted by Eurostar (UK) for maintenance, it is still the driver's responsibility to ensure that the train is completely safe and, like the pilot of an airline, the driver undertakes a whole series of pre-departure checks to ensure that all the equipment is functioning correctly. The check procedure is complicated by the fact that the train has been designed to operate over three (four if Eurotunnel's system in included) railway networks. This means that there are three different voltages to accommodate and two different types of power pick-up (the third rail and the two pantographs), as well as a multitude of differing signalling and safety systems. The driver will also be provided with documentation for the trip; this includes a route map (although few, except recently trained drivers will need to refer to this) and a 'Fiche Train', which provides the driver with a timetable illustrating the passing times at significant points along the route. This he will keep on the main controller to enable him to

refer to during the course of the journey.

Initially the driver will log into the system by selecting one of the operational languages and he will then follow a predetermined procedure for fault analysis and checking. Just as on an aircraft, the Eurostar trains are fitted with a 'black box' recorder and this will monitor the pre-departure check just as it will record the speed and operation of the train once it has departed. The first check involves examining the on-board computer's log; there are a number of pages here that record various types of faults and modifications. As the train has just come out of North Pole, there should be nothing, other than standard information about modifications logged. There is also a manual check book, which the driver will examine for any supplementary information. It will also be his responsibility to log any significant faults noted during the trip out to Paris to alert the crew that will return with the train to London. Following this check, the driver will undertake a detailed check of all of the various systems on board the train. It is his responsibility to ensure that all the relevant signalling and safety

equipment is functioning and he goes through each check, resetting the circuit breakers when they are tripped out. The train is also fitted with a radio that provides immediate access to the appropriate signalbox. This is also tested through a call to Wimbledon box, which will control the train's departure from Waterloo and the short stretch of the journey to the Stewarts Lane viaduct; contact is confirmed and Wimbledon box is also able to confirm both the train number (that will identify the train on the signal panels in the boxes between London and Folkestone) and the route (the train will be taking the main Channel Tunnel route — CTR1). One test that cannot be undertaken is the use of the headlights; these should be utilised in an emergency, but the regulations state that the headlight should not be illuminated for test purposes in an area where there are other train movements. Given the frequency of trains arriving at and departing from Waterloo's domestic platforms, there is

little chance of finding a suitable slot to undertake the test safely.

Once the programme of tests have been completed the driver is able to inform the train captain that all is correct and that the train is ready for boarding. With the information to hand, the platform staff are notified and an announcement is made over the public address system that the train is now ready to board. The announcement is made first in English, followed by French; it is one of the points of operational etiquette that the announcements are made first in the language of the country in which the train is located. There are a number of up escalators which provide access from the departure lounge to the platform and it is at the foot of these that a manual ticket check is completed.

On the platform the train crew, assisted by the platform staff, ensure that the passengers board the train quickly and efficiently and, whilst the passengers board, multilingual announcements are made requesting that all luggage be safely stowed away in the vestibules, to ensure that the gangways are kept clear, and that all stacked baggage is properly labelled.

The embarkation is swiftly completed and a few moments before the actual departure a further announcement is made informing passengers that the doors will shut automatically in a few minutes. For the passengers the scene is now set for three hours of relaxed travel across the English and continental countryside; for the crew the real work is about to begin.

With the doors shut and with a green signal allowing him to start, the driver gently eases the main controller forward. The Eurostar train has six 'dead-man' positions, and the driver must be depressing one of these positions the whole time the train is in motion or else the train will automatically come to a halt. Generally speaking, the driver will use the two foot pedals for this purpose; these pedals pivot and, every so often, there will be a bleep. The driver should quickly depress the pedals and return

them to the central point; again, should he fail to do so, the train will automatically stop.

The train's speed through International Junction and onto the main lines out of Waterloo will be relatively slow, but the driver will continue to accelerate out of the station and towards Vauxhall. At this point the train is travelling, usually, on the reversible Windsor line; this route is bidirectionally signalled to allow this manoeuvre to be safely accomplished. Shortly after Vauxhall the train will deviate from the Waterloo-Clapham Junction route and ascend the new line over the Stewarts Lane viaduct; this section, built specifically for Eurostar services, gives access to the main line out of Victoria towards Tonbridge.

Between London and the Channel Tunnel Eurostar services share the tracks with trains operating into and out of London; inevitably this can mean that, particularly in peak periods, progress may appear tardy. In an effort to ensure some form of flexibility of operation, there are two routes between London and the Tunnel — CTR1 and CTR2 — and either route

Below: With Battersea power station in the background, a Eurostar passes Factory Junction with the 10.23 Waterloo-Brussels on 13 January 1995.
Chris Wilson

can be followed depending on operational requirements. Driving the trains through the London suburbs and on into the Kent countryside is a skilled operation; not only does the driver have to cope with a 400m long train — considerably longer than other passenger trains encountered on the British side — but with numerous junctions, gradients and potentially adverse signals as the Eurostar service weaves its way towards the coast.

From the Stewarts Lane viaduct — where the train passes from the control of Wimbledon to London Victoria box — the train eases its way through Wandsworth Road and Clapham High Street stations, where commuters stand waiting for their next train into London, before passing through Brixton Junction, where the alternative route (CTR2) heads off towards Denmark Hill. The onward journey continues through Herne Hill, West Dulwich and Sydenham Hill. The train enters Penge Tunnel, a minnow at 1.25 miles in length in comparison to the Channel Tunnel, before passing through Penge East, Kent House, Beckenham Junction and Shortlands Junction. Following Bromley South

and Bickley the train takes the line towards Petts Wood at Bickley Junction; this was another section of route that was upgraded to accommodate Eurostar services. It is over this stretch of line that control of the train passes to the Ashford IECC.

Whilst our driver negotiates his way through the labyrinthine railway network of south London, the rest of the crew is also hard at work. Each train has two suitably qualified personnel to drive the train if necessary in an emergency in the Channel Tunnel, along with buffet staff and stewards to serve First-Class passengers. As this train is an early morning departure, passengers in First-Class accommodation will receive breakfast. Other departures, depending upon the actual time, will see First-Class passengers receive either lunch or dinner. For Standard-Class passengers two trolley services will operate, one in either of the Standard-Class sections. In addition, between the Standard and First-Class accommodation will be found two buffets. Normally the trolley is accompanied by two members of the train crew, one to serve the passenger and one to operate the hand-held

Below: Eurostar rake F8 (3217/8) passing Continental Junction at Dollands Moor with the 12.12 Paris-Waterloo train on 23 March 1995. Meanwhile SNCF Nos BB22401/5 await their next duty. *Chris Wilson*

calculator which enables the train crew to provide prices in pounds, French francs or Belgian francs. The actual staffing level on board the train will depend upon the number of passengers being carried.

In addition to the operational staff, there are also a number of officials whose position reflects the curious status of the international train. Legally speaking the train will remain under British law until the passengers have disembarked at Paris Gare du Nord (and in the reverse direction French law applies until arrival at Waterloo International). In case of any incident a policeman travels on the train and, if required, the train is also equipped with a secure cell in which any miscreant can be locked for the journey. Also on board are officials who will undertake the passport check prior to the train's arrival in Paris; passport checks for both Britain and France are now undertaken on the train; in Brussels, however, the Belgian authorities have retained the traditional passport control at Midi station.

The driver continues to press on towards the tunnel; for much of the time, given the power of the traction equipment (even allowing for the fact that only part of the available tractive effort is utilised when operating in third-rail mode), the train is largely coasting, with the driver giving gentle bursts of power to ensure a smooth ride over the gradients. Passing through Petts Wood and Orpington, the train breaks out into the Kent countryside as it passes through Polhill Tunnel and Dunton Green station. As the train progresses further from the congested track of the London suburban network, so the driver is able to increase the speed of the unit towards the maximum permitted on the UK side of the Tunnel; this speed is still far short of the maximum that will be achieved once the train has crossed over into France.

The train passes through Sevenoaks and Hildenborough before the driver is forced to decelerate on the approaches to the junction at Tonbridge. Passing through the station, the train accelerates again as it heads for Paddock Wood. Passing through the stations at Marden, Staplehurst, Headcorn (once the junction for the long-closed Kent & East Sussex Railway) and Pluckley, the next major junction to be

Above: An impressive sight as the mighty Eurostar enters the Channel Tunnel.

encountered is that at Ashford. This particular train is timetabled to stop at the new international station at Ashford, so the train is signalled into one of the platform roads. After a few minutes in the station, the doors are closed and the train is ready once again to depart. Immediately beyond the station the lines to Canterbury (left) and Hastings (right) head off.

Although not visible to the travelling public, the driver will be aware that the next level crossing, that at Willesborough, immediately after the junctions, is one of the many anachronisms of the British route to the Channel Tunnel. Alongside the track is a small hut where the crossing keeper maintains a vigil; this is the only manually-controlled level crossing between London and Paris and it is a sight that is often portrayed in the media as highlighting the differences between Britain and France in terms of railway investment. A more positive reflection of investment comes immediately afterwards with the disused sidings at Sevington; this was where the construction trains brought the raw materials that enabled the British half of the Channel Tunnel to be constructed.

The penultimate station on the British side of the Channel Tunnel is that at Westenhanger and, for the driver and crew, preparations need to be made for the entry into the tunnel. An announcement is made — the last on this particular journey that will be made in English first — that the train is about to enter the tunnel and that the journey time will be about 20min. A second driver makes his way to the rear driving compartment; it is one of the regulations for the use of the Channel Tunnel that a qualified driver must be stationed in the rear cab of the train so that, in the event of an emergency, the train can be reversed immediately. As an additional safety feature the Train Managers are also taught how to take over the controls of the train if necessary. Finally, the driver also has a hand-held radio for use in the event of the main train-signalling centre radio failing to operate. For the driver the immediate task is to make ready for the end of the third-rail section and the start of the 25kV route over Eurotunnel tracks.

Immediately after Westenhanger station and just before the train enters the 100yd-long Sandling tunnel, the driver will use one of the two switches that control the power supply and pick-up equipment. As the train approaches Sandling Tunnel the driver will switch the pick-up switch to '0'; this has the effect of retracting all the power collection equipment and results in the shoes for the third rail being raised. The train will coast for the two miles through Sandling station — the last station in Britain passed by Eurostar services — and the 954yd-long Saltwood Tunnel. As the train emerges from the latter, the driver will switch the second of the two switches from 'BR' (for Britain's third-rail) to 'ET' (Eurotunnel's 25kV system). He will then use the first switch to select 'N' to raise the normal 25kV pantographs.

The train passes from the Railtrack-owned Ashford-Folkestone main line to the Eurotunnel complex at Continental Junction. Immediately before the junction the driver will see the huge Dollands Moor terminal, through which the Channel Tunnel freight traffic is handled and, passing through Continental Junction, the huge expanse of the Eurotunnel site immediately becomes apparent. Eurostar services are timetabled to pass through the Channel Tunnel between Eurotunnel's own Le Shuttle services and freight traffic. The design of the Eurostar's cab was produced so that the potentially hypnotic strobe effect of the tunnels' concrete sections and lighting would be minimised. Whilst the train passes through the Channel Tunnel it is under the control of Eurotunnel's controllers at its Folkestone signalling centre. At the start of the tunnel the French TVM430 signalling system clicks in; this will effectively control the speed at which the train operates between the Cheriton portal and the outskirts of Paris.

'TVM' is an abbreviation of *Transmission Voie Machine* (which is translated as Track to Train Transmission) and is a reflection of the fact that, travelling at upto 300km/hr, the driver will be unable to utilise traditional lineside signalling equipment. The TVM430, which is situated at the front of the cab ahead of the main controller, consists of two rows of displays which are activated by coded track circuits. These circuits can identify the presence of the train and the distance that the train will take to stop. It will then indicate the maximum speed

Below: The local sheep don't seem to mind the noise of the train as it rushes through the countryside.

that the train can be driven at to ensure safe operation. In the event that the train is gaining on a slower moving or stationary train ahead, the TVM430 will show an ever decreasing maximum speed to which the driver must respond. The machine indicates the new lower speed limit one block section before it must be implemented. If the driver fails to respond by the start of the appropriate block section, the TVM430 will automatically apply the brakes.

On the TVM430 there are three distinct colours utilised. Displays with a green background indicate the maximum speed permitted over the line. Those with a black background show the maximum permitted speed for the train, whilst those with a white background are to provide the driver with a warning. As there are no anomalies with the TVM430 on this train our driver is able to validate the equipment.

The journey through the tunnel takes around 20min and, emerging onto French soil through the portal at the Portail de Beussingues, the driver will again need to reconfigure the power supply equipment to select the pantograph height used on the LGV route towards Lille and Paris. As before, the two power supply switches are used to ensure the safe retraction and realignment of the pantographs.

With the changeover safely accomplished the driver is able to accelerate towards Calais-Fréthun station. Again the immediate environment is dominated by the Eurotunnel terminal, but as the train accelerates away, the passenger will soon be whisked through the open countryside of northern France. The speed builds up rapidly as the train heads inland; shortly before the maximum line speed (300km/hr) is reached the driver notifies the Train Manager that this maximum speed will be achieved and this information is relayed to the passengers over the public address system.

The Eurostar services from Calais take the LGV-Nord Europe and this lacks the intermediate stations that were such a feature of the trip across England. For the driver the task is to keep the train running to the schedule and to the speed permitted by the TVM430. Although the LGV is a recently engineered route, the track undulates considerably — a

Below: A Eurostar train rushing through the Kent countryside.

reflection of the high power to weight ratio of both the TGV and Eurostar sets that are designed to use it — and this means that the driver has to demonstrate considerable skill in ensuring both that any gradients are compensated for and that the speed limits are not exceeded. Although there are slight tolerances, should the driver exceed the maximum speed limit by more than a few km/hr then the train will brake automatically; the driver will also have to explain the excess speed when the computer record is verified.

The LGV route approaches Lille from the west and reaches the new Lille-Europe having crossed over conventional railway routes, seeming almost like a mild roller-coaster. The TVM430 indicates the speed for the trip through Lille — which this service does non-stop — and the driver decelerates to the permitted maximum. It is at Lille that the Eurostar services to Brussels depart northeastwards; until the completion of the fast

line to the Belgian capital, Eurostar services for Brussels deviate from the LGV-Nord Europe immediately to the east of Lille-Europe station and switch over to the conventional Lille-Froyennes route. This again requires drivers to switch power equipment from SNCF classic 25kV power supply to that for operation in Belgium to accommodate SNCB's 3,000V dc network.

These changes are, however, academic to the driver of a Paris-bound train as he accelerates away from Lille heading now almost due south towards Paris. Evidence of the construction of the high-speed line to Brussels is found some five miles south of Lille, where a new triangular junction will give access from the west towards Brussels for Eurostar services and from the south for the Thalys TGV services linking Paris, Brussels and Amsterdam.

The train is now on its final lap heading towards Paris; as with the journey between Calais and Lille the driver's task is to ensure

Above: Top speed is reached on the long straight sections in France.

Above: Journey's end: unlike the British and Belgian stations prepared for the Eurostar service, passengers arriving at the Gare du Nord in Paris used to face on occasions a long walk in the rain!
Colin Boocock

that the train travels smoothly over the rolling French landscape. Much of the route is alongside the main Paris-Lille motorway, but the speed of the road vehicles means that, in comparison with the 300km/hr achieved by the Eurostar trains, the cars and lorries look almost static. On the approaches to Paris there is a further triangular junction; this gives access to the LGV-Interconnexion, which is a high-speed line round the east of Paris that enables TGV sets to bypass Paris completely and link in to the LGV-Sud-Est.

As the train passes over this triangular junction, the driver has to prepare for the final reconfiguration of the pantograph as the train approaches the conventional SNCF network just to the north of the station at Villiers-le-Bel-Gonesse. The train is now some 15km from its final destination and, in a mirror image of its departure from London, these final few kilometres will see the train surrounded by numerous suburban services serving the communities on the north side of Paris. The stations of Garges and Pierrefitte-Stains are passed before a further junction brings the train through the large station of St Denis. Between St Denis and Gare du Nord, SNCF undertook major track reconstruction to enable both the Eurostar and the TGV services to reach their dedicated platforms at the extreme west side of Gare du Nord. As the train proceeds it continues to decelerate so that it is travelling at no more than a crawl as it passes the Eurostar depot in Paris, Le Landy, in which can be seen further Eurostar sets.

The Eurostar platforms at Gare du Nord, although converted from existing facilities (unlike London Waterloo) are physically separated from the rest of the station by glass screens. As the train arrives in the station promptly at 12.23 it pulls up at the buffer stops, providing those on the concourse with dramatic evidence of the arrival of another international train. With the doors released, the passengers can make their way along the train and out through the barriers; unlike London Waterloo, which has retained a customs examination area, there is direct access from the platform to the concourse. The observant passengers will have noted that, in comparison with the platforms at Waterloo, the platform at Gare du Nord is much lower, the discrepancy in height being accommodated by the appearance of an additional step at each door — another reflection of the differing standards of facilities that the Eurostar sets have to compensate for.

With the arrival in Paris, the trip is over for the passengers; for the train and crew, however, there is still much to do. The train-set will be cleaned, checked and restocked with food before forming a return working to London later in the afternoon. For the crew, too, there will be the opportunity for relaxation before the next group of passengers arrive, ready for their trip to Waterloo International. Upstairs, however, there are already passengers gathering in the Gare du Nord departure lounge eager for the 13.07 service to London. Another trainset, another crew, but the same efficiency of service and the same thrill of a high-speed run across Europe and through the Channel Tunnel.

Left: The concourse at Paris Gare du Nord; the Eurostar check-in facilities and departure lounge are located on the Mezzanine floor.

Left: Additional details from the facade of Paris Gare du Nord. The statues were designed by Cavalier to symbolise the principal cities served by trains from the Gare du Nord.

10 Hours in Paris, London and Brussels

PARIS

onfined within the limits of the Boulevard Périphérique, the city of Paris is remarkably compact, and very few of the world's great cities have kept and acknowledged the importance of their rivers down through history as Paris has done with the Seine. It is the main reference point of the city, with almost every building and landmark of importance either actually on the banks or nearby. An excellent way to enjoy this view and get a quick impression of this magnificent city is to take a cruise with one of the four companies that run services along the river: Bateaux-Mouches from Pont de l'Alma, Bateaux-Vedettes Pont Neuf from the Square du Vert-Galant, Vedettes de Paris Ile de France from Pont d'Iéna, and Bateaux Parisiens, also from Pont d'Iéna.

Navigating your way around Paris is very easy because of its compact size, plus it is well served with an excellent public transport system that is fast, reliable, and well-signposted. The Métro is the simplest and quickest way of moving around, with services that are more frequent than on the London Underground and stations that are closer together (the Parisian boast is that no point in the capital is more than 500m[550yd] from a station), making everything worth seeing within easy reach. Free maps are available at all stations. The bus service is similarly well endowed and gives the added advantage of much more to see. Tickets can be bought at any Métro station and can be used on both underground and buses. A similar system to the London Travelcard exists: the Formule 1 ticket which allows unlimited travel on tubes and buses. Alternatively, if you intend mainly to meander above ground *Un carnet* of 10 tickets (easily used if there are two of you) may suffice. If you do use the bus, remember to validate your ticket on entry (but don't if you have a Formule 1 ticket). The Métro lines are all numbered: make sure you know the station at the end of the line you want to use. It is this name that is signposted — eg Direction Porte D'Orléans.

Few cities can compare to Paris when it comes to restaurants, cafés and bars, that give it a worldwide gastronomic pre-eminence and reputation. By sitting in one of these unique establishments you can imbibe the true spirit of the city along with your refreshment, for the haughty and self-conscious Parisians live much of their lives in such public places.

Parisian museums and galleries are probably the best in Europe, with a long tradition of state cultural endowment, including The Louvre, Beaubourg, Musée d'Orsay and Cité des Sciences et de l'Índustrie. The commercial art galleries are found in three main areas: Rue de Seine and the adjoining streets of the Left Bank; round the Centre Pompidou; and along the Faubourg St-Honoré, Avenue Matignon, Rue de la Boëtie.

In keeping with the French treatment of cinema as an artform, Paris is also known as the cinema capital of the world, with a massive range of choice at any one time. It also possesses an exuberant music scene, both

Previous page: Trafalgar Square fountains. The National Gallery is on the left.

Right: One of the wonderful Art Nouveau Metro signs so characteristic of Paris.

Left: The Louvre contains one of the most important art collections in Europe, including such classics as the 'Mona Lisa' by Leonardo da Vinci. *Peter Waller*

Right The Hôtel de Ville is a 19th century reconstruction of an older building destroyed during the Paris Commune of 1871. The Mayor of Paris is one of the most important political figures in France.
Peter Waller

classical and contemporary, something to cater for almost any taste. All details of venues and programmes can be found in one of the listings magazines published each Wednesday and available at any news kiosk. They include *Pariscope*, *L'Officiel des Spectacles* and *Sept à Paris*. Above and apart from all its history and culture, Paris is perhaps most renowned for its shops, fashion and food, which combined together impart that particularly French ambience of style and form.

Here are a few ideas of how you could spend a day in Paris.

LA VOIE TRIOMPHALE

From Gare du Nord to Louvre Métro station. This walk stretches in an absolutely straight line from the eastern end of the Louvre to the Arc de Triomphe and could continue on to the modern complex of skyscrapers at La Défense, 9km (5.6 miles) away. The walk incorporates some of the city's most famous landmarks — across the Place de la Concorde, the Champs-Élysées, the Arc de Triomphe, the Musée du Louvre and the Tuileries. These huge monumental and ceremonial edifices were erected over the

centuries by kings and emperors, presidents and corporations, to glorify French power and prestige.

The Louvre — surely both Paris and France's most important and historic building, oozing history from its stonework. First constructed as a fortress in 1190, it was enlarged over the centuries by kings and emperors, and sacked several times by the mob in more revolutionary times. Its use changed over the centuries, from fortress to residential palace, treasure-house, archive, arsenal, artists' commune, and finally to a museum — the world's largest, housing one of the most important art collections ever gathered together.

Jardin des Tuileries — formal neo-classical gardens abundant in sculpture laid out initially by Catherine de' Medici, but later by Le Nôtre, revealing carefully conceived perspectives of the Louvre, the Place de la Concorde, and the Champs-Élysées. It is pleasant to sit in one of the outdoor cafés in the park and enjoy the views so carefully created. Running parallel to the gardens are two of the city's most famous (and expensive) shopping streets, the Rue de Rivoli and Rue St-Honoré.

Below:
Controversial when built, I. M. Pei's glass pyramid entrance to the Louvre Museum is now a tourist sight in its own right.

Right: The vista along the Champs-Élysées towards the Arc de Triomphe right in the heart of Paris.

La Place de la Concorde — This is massive and magnificent, with carefully conceived and executed perspectives in every direction — Gabriel's neo-classical mansions the Hôtel de la Marine and the Hôtel Crillon, the Champs-Élysées, the Tuileries and the Louvre, north to the Madeleine and south across the Pont de la Concorde over the river towards the Chambre des Députés. As befits the Triumphal Way, it has witnessed various historic events played out in its huge 8-hectare space. In 1792 the guillotine was set up here, and it was only at the end of the Reign of Terror that the square was given its present name. The obelisk comes from the famous temple at Luxor, and was given to King Louis-Philippe by a viceroy of Egypt in 1829. 3,300 years old, 23m (75ft) tall and weighing approximately 250 tonnes, it records the achievements of Pharaoh Rameses II.

Les Champs-Élysées — The most famous avenue in Paris, scene of national parades since Napoleon's body was brought home from St Helena in 1840, it leads to the ceremonial heart of the capital: the Arc de Triomphe. Laid out by Le Nôtre in 1667 it became the fashionable place to ride or stroll and be seen in. Cafés, restaurants, theatres and music all combined to make it the symbol of the *Belle Époque* and the sophisticated Parisian lifestyle. On one side are the Grand and Petit Palais, built for the World Exhibition in 1900, and now a museum and cultural centre, and on the other the Elysée Palace, residence of the President.

L'Arc de Triomphe — Sited in the Place Charles de Gaulle — a star with 12 avenues radiating from its centre, chosen by Napoleon to be the site of a triumphal arch celebrating the victories of the French (and his) army. It is an impressive 50m high and 45m wide. In 1920 an unidentified soldier killed in World War 1 was ceremonially buried under the Arch, and an eternal flame on his tomb has been kept burning ever since. At its top, an observation deck gives marvellous views of the city.

SACRÉ-COEUR — MONTMARTRE

Easily walkable. Out of Gare du Nord into Place Napoleon III. Onto Blvd de Magenta, heading north. Turn left onto Blvd Rochechouart, and then the fifth turning on the right Rue de Steinkerque. At the top of this street begins the steps and gardens climbing to the Sacré-Coeur Basilica.

This area, known as the Butte, still retains the feel of a village, its little streets winding up the hill of Montmartre, with Pigalle at its feet. The Paris Commune began here after the Franco-Prussian war of 1870-71, and the Basilica was started in 1875, and consecrated in 1919, although services were held there in the 1890s. It was in the 19th century that Montmartre became the intellectual and artistic centre of the capital, attracting artists and writers, painters and poets to its cheap bohemian atmosphere. Circles and café-groups grew, the Moulin Rouge, the Chat Noir, the Moulin de la Galette added a musical and glamorous sparkle as the area became a floating world of art, spectacle and ideas. Utrillo, Toulouse-Lautrec, Caran d'Ache, Andre Gill, Berlioz, Nerval, Murger, Heine, Picasso, Braque and Gris; over a period of 40 years (1871-1914) Montmartre was pre-eminent, at last giving way to Montparnasse and becoming a place of more mundane entertainment.

BEAUBOURG — LES HALLES

From Gare du Nord take the Métro or RER Lines B or D to Châtelet-les-Halles. The city's first food market was on the Île de la Cité, but was settled on the site of Les Halles from the 12th century onwards. By the 19th century the great market was urgently in need of renovation, and so between 1854 and 1866, 10 great halls were built. Almost a 100 years later, the city had outgrown the capacity of this grand old market area so full of character and ambience. In 1968, through Georges Pompidou, the then president, the whole area was transformed into a new multi-purpose multi-level shopping complex and leisure centre, with direct Métro access. Included in it are museums, art-galleries, cinemas, shopping malls, cafés, childrens play areas, tree-lined walkways, fountains, sculpture, frescos, mosaic columns and terrace areas from which to view the whole complex.

From Les Halles one naturally gravitates to the futuristic Pompidou Centre, a building inverted, with its insides on the outside. This multipurpose cultural centre has weathered the storm of its beginning to become one of the best loved and most visited buildings in Paris.

Below: Sacré-Cœur dominates the hills around Montmartre, the favourite district for artists and bohemians in Paris.

Above: One of the many portrait artists in the Place du Tertre, Montmartre.

Included inside are the Industrial Design Centre, the Public Information Library, the Institute of Acoustic and Musical Research, and last but not least the world-famous National Museum of Modern Art. Outside, the open piazza has become popular for improvised culture of every kind, and large crowds gather to watch the street performers. The café and restaurant on the top of the centre provide a superb panorama of the city.

HÔTEL DE VILLE — ÎLE DE LA CITÉ

Gare du Nord to Châtelet. The Hôtel de Ville is the official reception and city council building. The present version is a 19th century reconstruction of a 17th century Town Hall burned down by the revolutionaries of the Paris Commune in 1871, it thus reflects the turbulent history of the city. Opponents of the kings and emperors created their municipal governments here in 1789, 1848 and 1870. After the Paris Commune the Bourgeoisie suppressed all municipal authority, and for 100 years Paris was ruled directly by the government. The most recent head of an independent municipality was Jacques Chirac who became the first elected mayor of Paris in over a century.

Crossing the Pont D'Arcole leads from the Hôtel de Ville onto the Île de la Cité. It was here that the city first began, with Celtic tribes making a settlement on the island; one tribe, the Parisii, were eventually to give their name to the city. Despite Haussmann's almost complete modernisation the Île still reflects the ancient medieval heart of the capital, and of the country. Its main sights are listed below:

Sainte Chapelle — A Gothic chapel, hailed as one of the great architectural masterpieces of the western world, it features 15 stunning stained-glass windows 15m (50ft) high, portraying more than 1,000 Biblical scenes in fantastic colour.

The Conciergerie — Part of the Palais de Justice. It was originally a prison, and retains its 11th century torture chamber, the Bonbec

Tower, and a 14th century clock tower. During the Revolution as many as 12,000 men and women were held here at one time, and during the Reign of Terror the building was the ante-chamber of the Tribunal. In all almost 3,000 prisoners left the Conciergerie for the guillotine.

Notre Dame — The most famous building in Paris, and a masterpiece of French art. Built on the site of a Roman temple, work began in 1163, but it took 200 years to finally bring the project to fruition. It was finally finished in 1345, though none of the original plans had been changed. It has witnessed the great events of French history ever since.

TROCADÉRO — EIFFEL TOWER — MUSÉE D'ORSAY — LATIN QUARTER

Gare du Nord to Eiffel Tower. The Chaillot Palace, Trocadéro Gardens, and the Eiffel Tower form a striking and complete early 20th century group. Across the Pont d'Iéna on the North Bank lies the Chaillot Palace, and the Trocadéro Gardens, with the semi-circular Place du Trocadéro behind it, an equestrian statue of Marshal Foch in its centre. The low-lying white stone palace was built in 1937, consisting of two winged pavilions linked by a portico curving to frame a wide terrace. Within it are the Maritime Museum, the Museum of French Monuments and the Museum of Mankind. Beneath the terrrace is the Chaillot National Theatre, and then a large pool with fountains that is spectacularly floodlit at night. On either side of this central pool the Trocadéro Gardens fall towards the River Seine. The name Trocadéro was given to this area in 1827 to commemorate the French capture of the Trocadero fort near Cadiz.

Eiffel Tower — The capital's ultimate viewing platform and best known monument. When it was built it was the tallest building in the world, though now greatly surpassed. Its total height with the addition of a television mast is 320m (1,051ft), its weight 7,000 tonnes.

Left: The great Gothic cathedral of Notre Dame on the Île de la Cité.

It was erected for the First World Trade Fair in 1889, by Gustav Eiffel, its daring engineer, but it was initially strongly opposed — over 300 celebrities and people of importance signed a petition in an attempt to prevent it. But up it went, and when in 1909 the concession ended it had achieved acceptance, and remained. It has three platforms, the first two containing restaurants and on the third a bar. There are lifts up to the top, but also 1,652 steps for the fit and brave.

Musée d'Orsay — Built in 1898-1900 by Laloux, as the Parisian terminus of the Orléans line, in the 1970s it narrowly avoided demolition. In 1986 it reopened as the Musée d'Orsay, dedicated to 19th century art.

Latin Quarter — Named originally after the Latin spoken by students at the university, founded in 1215, and along with Bologna the oldest in Europe. The Sorbonne is still the natural centre of this charming area, with its maze of narrow cobbled streets, filled with bookshops, art galleries and cafés. Even though the more affluent continue to penetrate, this is still an area for the young and radical to congregate, and continue the Left Bank traditions of art, philosophy and politics.

Right: The view that means Paris the world over — the Eiffel Tower, built for the World Fair in 1889. At the time it was the tallest building in the world at 300m (984ft). On a clear day you can see for 67km (42 miles) from the top, which is reached in three stages in the ancient, original lifts.

LONDON

As with all of the world's largest and capital cities it was its river, the Thames, which brought about the rise of London. Liquid history — a cliché, and yet like all clichés true. London sprawls in a clay basin with a surrounding rim of low hills, 40 miles from the river's mouth. The Thames flows from west to east across the city, roughly dividing it into two halves, the northern part being the more important for the tourist and sightseer.

Seldom deliberately planned, there has never been a tyrant or mastermind to oversee the development of this great city, just the gradual random development and growth over the ages. As its borders extended, small villages and towns were absorbed or joined up into the huge conglomeration. Still today London has the feel of many distinct parts merging to form the whole. Though it seems at times that it has turned its back on the river that made it, yet much of London and its history can be viewed from the Thames, and it is to the river that the sightseer should first venture.

London has many cheap transport schemes, but for the one-day tourist the best is a Travelcard which allows unlimited use of bus, suburban trains and Underground. The only caution is that it should cover all the zones (numbered areas radiating out from the centre) you are likely to use. The Underground lines are all colour keyed and identify direction by cardinal points — eg Bakerloo Line Northbound.

HOUSES OF PARLIAMENT — BIG BEN — WESTMINSTER ABBEY and RIVER CRUISE TO THE THAMES BARRIER

Route from Waterloo International station: Bakerloo or Northern Line one stop to Embankment station, then District or Circle Line one stop to Westminster station.

Left: The Palace of Westminster, designed by Charles Barry and Augustus Pugin, it was completed in 1852 to replace the old palace which had burnt down 18 years earlier.

Right: The imposing frontage of Selfridges department store in Oxford Street.

Far right: 51m (170ft) above London stands Admiral Horatio Nelson on top of his 16 ton Corinthian column in Trafalgar Square. The statue was designed by Baily, the pedestal by Railton, while guarding him at the base are Landseer's grand lions.

At Westminster station, one emerges out of the Underground into Parliament Square. The Houses of Parliament, Big Ben and the Abbey of Westminster are all immediately visible. The Houses of Parliament are open to the public when in session: both the House of Lords and the House of Commons have visitors' galleries with free admission. In 1834 most of the Palace of Westminster including the Houses of Parliament burnt down, and were replaced by the present neo-Gothic structure designed by Charles Barry and Augustus Pugin. Westminster Abbey, a superb example of medieval architecture with many English kings buried inside, and the clock tower containing Big Ben are just alongside.

After looking at the political centre of the capital and the country, one can take a cruise from Westminster pier, either down-river to the Thames Barrier, or upstream to Kew and Hampton Court Palace. Downriver one can alight at the Tower of London and Tower Bridge (30min), Greenwich Observatory and National Maritime Museum (45min), or the Thames Flood Barrier itself (75min). This journey unfolds riverside London, with all the historic buildings and monuments on the way, often entertainingly pointed out and explained by the captain of the riverboat.

OXFORD STREET — REGENT STREET — TOTTENHAM COURT ROAD — PICCADILLY — SOHO

Route from Waterloo: Bakerloo Line four stops to Oxford Circus.

From Oxford Circus walk down Regent Street to Piccadilly Circus, and from there five minutes further down Piccadilly to the Royal Academy art gallery. Alternatively walk down Oxford Street itself, to the Marble Arch end where various department stores, such as Selfridges, are clustered, or towards Centrepoint and Tottenham Court Road. You can turn off right at any time and get into Soho, with its little cafés, restaurants, wine bars and markets. Behind Tottenham Court Road lies the huge British Museum with its magnificent collections of ancient and historic artefacts. This whole area is perhaps the main shopping and entertainment centre of London, filled with every kind of shop and market to cater for every taste — from the expensive and exclusive to the cheap and cheerful. One can wander for hours

Turning back, walk past Charing Cross station and down the Strand. By cutting up left one arrives in Covent Garden, originally the home of the old fruit and vegetable markets. Now the market's beautiful old iron and stone buildings have been renovated and converted into one of the city's premier shopping and entertainment areas, extremely popular with tourists and Londoners alike. Within this area are restaurants, theatres, wine bars, boutiques, shops and museums, including the Royal Opera House, and the theatre and transport museums. In the piazza, people gather to watch public performers, or enjoy a drink and a meal at one of the outside tables of the popular cafés that ring the old market area.

Below: One of the decorative name plates high above the crowds in Oxford Street at Oxford Circus.

choosing a random route to find unexpected delights in the backstreets. With the use of a London guide, such as the *A-Z Streetfinder*, to orient yourself, it is easy to make the most of this labyrinthine area.

CHARING CROSS — TRAFALGAR SQUARE — COVENT GARDEN

Route from Waterloo: Northern or Bakerloo Line two stops to Charing Cross. Charing Cross is the official centre of London. Behind the equestrian statue of Charles I a bronze plaque was set into the pavement in 1955, from which mileages are measured. Turning left one comes into Trafalgar Square, built to celebrate Nelson's famous naval victory. The Admiral stands on his huge column in the centre, from where looking through the Admiralty Arch down The Mall one can catch sight of Buckingham Palace. On one side is the National Gallery, comprising one of the richest and most extensive art collections in the world. Opposite is Whitehall, leading to Parliament Square, passing government offices and Downing Street on the way.

KING'S ROAD — KENSINGTON — KNIGHTSBRIDGE — HARRODS

Route from Waterloo: Bakerloo or Northern line one stop to Embankment, then Circle or District Line four stops to Sloane Square, or five stops to South Kensington.

If it's shopping you want, then take a trip to the world's most famous department store — Harrods, where it used to be said that you could buy anything, including an elephant. Take a look at the exotic wares in its gorgeously tiled food hall. Harrods is a short bus trip away from Sloane Square where the King's Road can be joined, and the Royal Court Theatre is to be found. The King's Road contains a mixture of fashionable boutiques and wonderful antique shops. From Sloane Square or Knightsbridge tube stations you can travel to South Kensington to visit the Science, Natural History, Geological, and the Victoria and Albert Museums — the latter is the national museum of fine and applied arts of all countries.

THE TOWER OF LONDON — TOWER BRIDGE — HMS *BELFAST* — LONDON DUNGEONS — THE GLOBE

Route from Waterloo station: Bakerloo or Northern Line one stop to Embankment, then six stops eastwards on the District or Circle Line to Tower Hill station.

Below: The Horse Guards trotting through London make a colourful and exciting spectacle.

Coming up out of Tower Hill station the Tower of London is immediately visible. It is one of the most imposing fortresses in Britain, steeped in blood and history, and a garrison, a palace, a mint, an armoury, a museum and a prison at different times in its past. The oldest part is the White Tower, built by William the Conqueror, where are kept the Crown Jewels in their subterranean Jewel House. The entrance to the Tower from the river is called Traitors' Gate through which prisoners were led to their execution — and there were many executions, for the Tower has been intimately connected with the darker side of English history.

From the Tower one can stroll to Tower Bridge, London's most famous and spectacular bridge, built between 1886-1894 by Horace Jones and John Wolfe Barry. Its Gothic towers house the steel structure that carries the bridge mechanism. The two drawbridges weigh 1,000 tonnes each, and the two walkways connecting the tops of the towers are 43m (142ft) above high-water level, offering superb views of the city. The bridge also has its own museum.

Once over the bridge turn right and walk upstream to HMS *Belfast*, a World War 2 cruiser of 11,500 tonnes. Commissioned in 1939 she saw action throughout the war, and opened the D-Day bombardment prior to the landings in 1944. She is now a floating museum, and her seven decks can be explored to give a vivid impression of what it was like to live and fight at sea.

A little further upstream on the same bank are the London Dungeons, featuring gruesome exhibits of the city's blood-curdling past — sacrifices, plagues, tortures, murders and executions. Not for the faint-of-heart! Beyond this, near the now disused Bankside power station, is the newly-built and opened reconstruction of Shakespeare's original Globe Theatre.

Below: It is possible to go up onto the high level footbridge of Tower Bridge to get wonderful river views of London. It was built in 1894 by Horace Jones and John Wolfe Barry. The drawbridges are still operated to allow large ships to pass through — the times when this happens are displayed by the ticket office.

BRUSSELS

A federal country with three official languages and an intense regional rivalry and competition, Belgium has a cultural excitement and diversity that belies its dull reputation. Marking the border and meeting point of the Flemish and Walloon parts of the country, the capital Brussels, is central enough to be unavoidable from any direction. A culturally varied city, it is far more interesting than its reputation as Euro-capital would suggest (it became the headquarters of the EEC in 1959). Brussels can be used as a base from which to explore elsewhere in this small country. Its architecture and museums rank with the best of Europe's capitals, with a well-preserved medieval centre and vibrant street and nightlife.

One of the most striking aspects of the city is the sharp contrast between the internationalism of the central and EEC zones which are somewhat nondescript, full of business, governmental and administrative complexes, with that of the vital foreign and immigrant quarters. The compact nature of Brussels only serves to heighten this feeling as you step from one extreme to the other — from a slum to an upmarket square of shops and cafés.

The city's wealth and class divides are manifested in its very layout. Since the 11th century royalty and the wealthy have lived in the Upper Town, and the poor and working class in the Lower Town, with the linguistic and cultural chasms of the country concentrated likewise. The city has been officially bilingual since 1962, and by law all street and traffic signs and public information must be in both Flemish and French.

Brussels is very cosmopolitan with the EEC headquarters and its African and Mediterranean immigrants: all these communities live separate

Below: Brussels is a marvellous place to eat, with a wide range of ethnic restaurants from which to choose.

lives side-by-side, which only makes the city more intriguing. Renowned for its bars and restaurants and food rivalling Paris — an astonishing variety — ethnic, trendy, élite, traditional and basic, Brussels possesses some wonderful markets, *chocolatiers*, shops, art galleries and antiques. The battlefield of Waterloo and the Museum of Central African Art are both close to the city, and easily accessible on public transport.

THE LOWER TOWN

The commercial heart of the city, with major shops, hotels and restaurants. The old market Grand' Place is the centre of this area. A square of stunning renovated buildings with the gilded façades of baroque guildhouses and the intricate Gothic Hôtel de Ville, this square is the obvious starting point for the exploration of the Lower Town.

To the north of Grand' Place is a maze of cobbled streets named after the produce that was once sold there — Rues du Beurre, des Bouchers, Marché aux Herbes, Fromages and Poulets, still medieval in their style and feel. With the building of the town hall in the 15th century the square became more the civic and political centre. Official decrees were read here,

and executions were carried out — the majority of them Protestants who had rebelled against the oppressive Catholic regime of Philip II. The real glory of the square are the guildhouses, exuberantly decorated and self-aggrandising. On the northern side is the Maison du Roi, a reconstructed Gothic building now housing the Musée de la Ville de Bruxelles and containing an excellent history of the city. Just beyond the Maison du Roi is Le Pigeon, the house in which Victor Hugo lived during his exile from France. He was expelled because of his support of the French insurrection of 1848.

On the opposite side of the square is Le Cygne — a bar where Karl Marx would meet Fredrich Engels, where they wrote the *Communist Manifesto*, and were expelled the following month! Next door is the Maison des Brasseurs — the only house still owned by its original guild, the brewers, and now the home of the Brewery Museum. Also close to the square are two of the city's favourite tourist attractions — the Musée de Costume et de la Dentelle on the Rue de la Violette, with fine examples of ancient and contemporary lace, and the Manneken Pis, on the Rue de l'Étuve, a famous statue of a little boy urinating.

Another sight in the Lower Town worth a visit include the Centre Belge de la Bande

Dessinée — a museum dedicated to the Belgian comic strip on the Rue des Sables, in the city's only surviving Horta-designed department store called Magasins Waucqez, worth a visit for the building alone, though Tin Tin fans will want to see the contents as well.

Right: The Manneken Pis on the rue de l'Etuve has little costumes especially made for it to celebrate various feast days and important events.

Below right: The Grand' Place is one of the best preserved city squares to be found anywhere with its amazing architecture and elaborately gilded buildings.

THE UPPER TOWN

On the gentle slope of the Upper Town sits the city's Cathedral, dedicated jointly to Saint Michel and Sainte Gudule the patron and patroness of Brussels, though more often known as the church of Ste Gudule. Like so much of the city it was badly damaged in the Restoration, and 100 years later by French artillery. Close to the Cathedral is the Palais de la Nation, and then the Parc de Bruxelles which possesses its own theatre.

Walking through the park one arrives at the neo-classical Place Royale, filled with mansions of rich aristocrats. In the centre of the square is an equestrian statue of Ste Godfrey, a crusader who became the first Christian King of Jerusalem. Round the square are the Palais Royal and both the Palais and the Musée des Beaux Arts, the Palais containing a theatre, a concert hall and a temporary exhibition centre. The sombre Palais Royal was built in 1904, the Belgian Royal dynasty being relatively very young —it was founded in 1831. Although this is their official residence they reside elsewhere and consequently the palace is open to visitors in August, when the luxurious rooms hung with superb tapestries, and collections of furniture, porcelain and glass can be seen. Across from

the Royal Palace is the Musée des Beaux Arts, featuring the Musée d'Art Moderne and the Musée d'Art Ancien. The Musée d'Art Moderne is certainly the city's most innovative, with an excellent collection laid out on eight underground levels.

Walking down Rue de la Régence one comes first to the Place du Petit Sablon, formerly a horse market; in 1890 it was laid out as a park and decorated with 48 statues representing the city's medieval guilds. On the other side of the square is the Palais Egmont, built in 1548 for Françoise of Luxembourg, mother of Count Egmont — who was executed for his opposition to the Spanish Tyranny. It was rebuilt in 1750 and again in the 1890s. On the next corner of the park is the Musée Instrumental du Conservatoire Royal de Musique, which houses an exquisite collection of musical instruments, ranging from mini-violins to inlaid and painted keyboards. There is also a display dedicated to Adolphe Sax, the inventor of the saxophone, which includes some of his more bizarre inventions, such as the saxhorn. This neighbourhood of Sablon is one of the wealthiest districts in Brussels, and is filled with expensive antique and art shops.

Further up the Rue de la Régence is the colossal Palais de Justice, towering above everything else. This is the city's most exclusive shopping area, full of designer boutiques, jewellers and *parfumiers.*

Left: The Grand' Place is the commercial hub of the city as evidenced by the merchant guilds who built their headquarters there centuries ago.

Eurostar

WHAT'S ON WHEN YOU GET OFF . . .

Date(1)	Event	Location	Terminal
January	Furniture Show	Köln (Cologne), Germany	Cologne
January	Motor Show	Bruxelles / (Brussels)	Brussels Midi
January - March	Rugby Internationals	UK / France	All
January	Fashion Shows	Paris	Paris Nord
January	World of Drawings & Watercolours Fair	London	Waterloo International
January	Film Festival	Bruxelles / (Brussels)	Brussels Midi
February	Carnival Europe	Nice, France	Paris Nord & Lille
February	Ambiente International Fair	Frankfurt, Germany	Frankfurt
February - March	Fine Art & Antiques Fair	London	Waterloo International
March	ABN Amro Tennis Tournament	Rotterdam, Holland	Brussels Midi
March	European Fine Art Fair	Maastricht, Holland	Brussels Midi
March	Chelsea Design Week	London	Waterloo International
March	Gold Cup (horse racing)	Cheltenham, UK	Waterloo International
March	Arts & Antiques Fair	Düsseldorf, Germany	Düsseldorf
March	International Art Fair	Frankfurt, Germany	Frankfurt
March - May	Keukenhof Bulb Gardens	Lisse, Holland	Brussels Midi
March	International Book Fair	Bruxelles / (Brussels)	Brussels Midi
March	Grand National (horse racing)	Manchester, UK Liverpool, UK	
March	Tours of the Royal Greenhouses, Laeken		Brussels Midi
April	Oxford v. Cambridge University Boat Race (rowing)	London	Waterloo International
April	Brocante Fair	Maastricht	Brussels Midi
April	Open Weekend in the Châteaux of the Médoc	The Médoc Region, France	Paris Nord
April	International Antiques Fair	Birmingham, UK	Birmingham, UK
April	Art & Antiques Fair	Hanover, Germany	Frankfurt, Germany
April	Marathon	Paris	Paris Nord
April	The Queen's Birthday celebrations & open-air markets	Throughout Holland	Brussels Midi
April	Brocante Fair	Ghent, Belgium	Brussels Midi & Lille-Europe
April	International Guitar Festival	Bruxelles / (Brussels)	Brussels Midi
April	Music Festival	Poitiers, France	Paris Nord
May	Open International Tennis Championship	Hamburg, Germany	Brussels Midi
May	British Antiques Dealers Association Fair	London	Waterloo International
May	Film Festival	Cannes, France	Paris Nord & Lille-Europe
May	National Windmill Open Day	Throughout Holland	Brussels Midi & Lille-Europe

116

Date(1)	Event	Location	Terminal
May	Sand Sculpture Festivals	Scheveningen, Holland	Brussels Midi & Lille-Europe
May	Art Festival	Bruxelles / (Brussels)	Brussels Midi
May	Brocante Fair	Lille, France	Lille-Europe
May	International Sailing Events	La Rochelle	Fréthun (Calais) & Paris Nord
May	Opera Festival	Glyndebourne, UK	Waterloo International & Ashford International
May	Chelsea Flower Show	London	Waterloo International
May - June	French Open Tennis Championships	Paris	Paris Nord
June	The Derby (horse racing)	Epsom, UK	Waterloo International
June - August	Test Matches (cricket)	Various locations, UK	UK Eurostar Terminals
June	Grosvenor House Antiques Fair	London	Waterloo International
June	Trooping the Colour (military parade)	London	Waterloo International
June	Le Mans 24-hr Race (motor racing)	Le Mans, France	Lille-Europe & Paris Nord
June	Royal Ascot (horse racing)	Ascot, UK	Waterloo International
June	Day of Music	Throughout Paris	Paris Nord
June	Festival de Musique Ancienne	Lyon, France	Lille-Europe & Paris Nord
June - July	Lawn Tennis Championship, Wimbledon	London	Waterloo International
June	House & Garden Fair	London	Waterloo International
June - July	International Film Festival	La Rochelle, France	Frethun (Calais) & Paris Nord
June - July	Jazz Festival	Glasgow, UK	Glasgow
June - August	Schleswig-Holstein Music Festival	Hamburg, Germany	Brussels Midi
June	The Queen's Cup (polo)	Windsor, UK	Waterloo International
July	Opera Festival	München (Munich), Germany	Frankfurt
July	Royal Regatta (rowing)	Henley, UK	Waterloo International
July	Tour de France (cycling)	Throughout France	All French Eurostar Terminals
July	Giant Flea Market	Bruges, Belgium	Lille-Europe & Brussels Midi
July	Hampton Court Palace Flower Show	Hampton Court, UK	Waterloo International
July	North Sea Jazz Festival	The Hague, Holland	Brussels Midi
July	Benson & Hedges Cup Final (cricket)	London	Waterloo International
14th July	Bastille Day (national holiday)	Throughout France	All French Eurostar Terminals
July - August	Henry Wood Promenade Concerts	London	Waterloo International
July	Special Visits to the Royal Palace	Bruxelles / (Brussels)	Brussels Midi
July - August	Early Music Festival	Bruges, Belgium	Lille-Europe & Brussels Midi
August	Antiques Fair	Birmingham, UK	Birmingham
August	Celtic Festival	Lorient, France	Paris Nord
August	Cowes Week (sailing)	Isle of Wight, UK	Waterloo International
August	International Festival	Edinburgh, UK	Edinburgh

Eurostar

Date(1)	Event	Location	Terminal(2)
August	Giant Flea Market	Bruges, Belgium	Lille Europe & Brussels Midi
August	Open air canal concert	Amsterdam	Brussels Midi
August	Notting Hill Carnival	London	Waterloo International
August	Tapis des Fleurs (carpet of flowers), Grand' Place	Bruxelles / (Brussels)	Brussels Midi
September	Fashion Shows	Paris	Paris Nord
September	NatWest Trophy Final (cricket)	London	Waterloo International
September	National Heritage Day	Throughout Belgium	Lille-Europe & Brussels Midi
September	National Heritage Days (10,000 monuments open to the public)	Throughout France	All French Eurostar Terminals
September - October	Oktoberfest (Festival)	München (Munich), Germany	Frankfurt
September	Giant Flea Market	Bruges, Belgium	Brussels Midi & Lille-Europe
October	Book Fair	Frankfurt, Germany	Frankfurt
October	Perfume Fair	Bruxelles / (Brussels)	Brussels Midi
October	Arts Festival	Lille, France	Lille-Europe
October	Grand Prix de l'Arc de Triomphe (horse racing)	Paris	Paris Nord
October	Motor Show	Berlin	Brussels Midi
October	International Arts Fair	Bruxelles / (Brussels)	Brussels Midi
November	RAC Veteran Car Run	London - Brighton	Waterloo International & Ashford International
November	Fine Arts & Antiques Fair, Olympia	London	Waterloo International
November	International Art Fair	Köln (Cologne), Germany	Köln
November	Christmas Markets	All over Germany	Brussels Midi
December	Brocante Fair, Grand Palais	Lille, France	Lille-Europe
December	European Christmas Markets, Sablon	Bruxelles / (Brussels)	Brussels Midi
December	Christmas Markets	All over Belgium	Brussels Midi & Lille-Europe

(1) Specific dates vary — always check with the relevant tourist board

Left: Crazy fountains near Paris's Pompidou Centre.

Chapter 6

The Future

Channel Tunnel Fire

When the Channel Tunnel was designed and built, the consortium had to consider a whole range of potential incidents — from the likelihood of rabid animals making their way through the tunnels (thereby avoiding Britain's rigid rabies controls) to the threat of international terrorism. Safety was one of the company's primary concerns, particularly given the fact that traffic through the tunnel would come from a variety of sources — the Eurostar services from London to Paris or Brussels, the through rail freight services, Eurotunnel's car shuttles and, last but by no means least, the Eurotunnel freight shuttles. Certain types of freight traffic were banned from the outset because of the perceived danger and, in the event of an incident, rigorous safety systems were introduced.

Whilst the risk of fire was one that had been recognised — and the tunnel had to receive clearance from both French and British fire brigades before it opened to the public — experience from other long-distance tunnels was that the risk was minimal. However, on 18 November 1996, a mid-evening freight shuttle from Calais to Folkestone entered the tunnel just before 10.00 French time. Loaded with 29 HGVs, the shuttle should have been a perfectly routine train; however — and the exact circumstances have yet to be finally identified (the French authorities appearing to ascribe the outbreak to arson linked to a lorry-drivers' strike) — one of the HGVs on board was on fire.

Although the incident was undoubtedly horrific for those involved, two things did emerge. Firstly, the presence of the service tunnel ensured that the train crew and HGV drivers were safely evacuated; at the time of construction the consortium was criticised for the additional cost of the service tunnel but this incident and training exercises have proved conclusively its merits. Secondly, although there were undoubted problems which have been highlighted in the subsequent enquiries, Eurotunnel's systems worked. In the light of the incident, and of the various reports, Eurotunnel has modified its operational manuals, confirming that safety remains its paramount concern.

For Eurostar, the effects of the tunnel fire were immediate; its raison d'être had — at least — temporarily disappeared since, with the inevitable and enforced closure (however limited) of the tunnel, through services could not operate. It could not have happened at a worse time; Eurostar had been promoting itself heavily in the pre-Christmas period and these plans were thrown into confusion. One wag suggested that one use for the equipment was to construct a Santa's grotto at North Pole depot and use the TMSTs for a shuttle service between Waterloo and North Pole; at least it had the right sort of Christmas ring to it!

Fortunately, the fire had damaged only one of the running tunnels and, after a two-week period of investigation, through passenger services were permitted to resume through the one complete bore and through the undamaged part of the second. Eurostar was able to operate 90% of its timetabled services. Whilst these services operated, Eurotunnel would rebuild the damaged section; full services were reintroduced on 1 June 1997. The strength of the Eurostar product is such that, even under the constraints imposed by reduced capacity through the tunnel, business has returned quickly after the fire and new records continue to be achieved.

Future Developments

The High Speed line in Belgium

With great commitment of resources for such a small country, Belgium's high-speed line is due for completion during 1998. When this and the CTRL in England are completed, it will take just 2 hours to travel London-Brussels — a journey time saving of 30min. A similar time for Paris-Brussels is anticipated.

The start of track laying was marked by a ceremony on 3 October 1995. At the time of writing, the first section — from the French border to Antoing is nearing completion.

The high speed link with the French TGV Nord line was designed to cope with:

- Eurostars
- Thalys
- Réseau TGV between Belgium and Brittany, the Alps and the Mediterranean without stopping in Paris
- ICE from Germany after the year 2000

The 71km (44 miles) high-speed line will run between the French border and Tubize. Beyond Tubize the existing line will be extended to four tracks. So Eurostar will be able to run at 220km/hr. Near Antoing the line will connect with the Tournai-Mons line, a key link to crossing the Walloon region.

The High Speed line to The Channel Tunnel through England

The CTRL will be one of the largest infrastructure projects in the UK over the latter part of the 1990s and is programmed to open in 2003. The cost is estimated to be c£3 billion which will include enabling works for Thameslink 2000 and for the widening of the M2 along the road from junctions 1-4 and any additional requirements which may be thrown up by the Hybrid Bill Select Committee.

Designed to be 108km long, 26km will be in tunnels. The London tunnels account for 20km; there will be a further 2.8km of twin-bore tunnel as the line passes under the Thames and another tunnel 3.2km of twin-track single-bore

tunnel under the North Downs. The track will be to the same gauge as the French TGV lines, enabling them to accommodate the French double-deck TGVs and high containers to improve freight potential. The tunnels will have ventilation shafts which will also serve as emergency access points at roughly 3km intervals.

There will be 145 structures on the surface including 11 viaducts — the largest being the crossing of the River Medway. Two new stations will be provided: Ebbsfleet and Stratford along with St Pancras. The plan is for traffic to run at speeds of up to 225kph proposed by Union Railways – but the design allows for increased speeds to 270km/hr with no greater noise than the 225kph originally planned. The line will also be able to take high speed freight services.

The projected timetable is:

December 1996	Royal Assent of Hybrid Bill
End 1997	Design work complete; start of construction
December 1998	London tunnel boring complete
June 2000	Thameslink enabling works complete
January 2001	All tunnel boring complete
January 2002	Trackwork complete
February 2002	St Pancras station completed
October 2002	All fixed equipment installations complete
March 2003	Issuance of permit to use after all testing complete
2003 onward	Connection to WCML and Stratford station opens

The New Route

Starting from St Pancras the route crosses the King's Cross Railway Lands before passing under the ECML and entering its 20km tunnel under London which will run under the North London Line corridor until it rises to reach a large retained cutting across the Stratford Railway Lands — the intended site for Stratford International. The railway will then continue in tunnel until it reaches Dagenham. At Dagenham the railway will have a junction with the old system for use by freight trains. It then runs along the existing Tilbury railway towards Purfleet then crosses the railway running alongside the Purfleet bypass to pass over the exit ramp from the Dartford Tunnel and under the northern approach to the QE2 bridge. There will then be a tunnel under the Thames close to the QE2 bridge between West Thurrock and Swanscombe in north Kent. Entering the Ebbsfleet valley it will reach the new station and a junction with the North Kent Railway. After leaving the valley the lines will cross under the A2 and there connect with the London-Chatham Railway — and the connecting line will carry Eurostar trains to Waterloo. The CTRL will then follow the A2/M2, crossing the Medway valley on a high viaduct before plunging through a 3km tunnel below the North Downs which will bring it out into the Boxley Valley to the north of Maidstone before it joins the M20 corridor. West of Ashford it will cross the M20 to reach Ashford and then follow the existing line to the tunnel, splitting to pass either side of Dollands Moor freight yard with a junction for freight trains before connecting with the Eurotunnel railway. The route will be controlled from a powerbox at Swanscombe. The Environmental Statement for the CTRL Bill assumed that by 2017 the CTRL will be carrying 150 outbound international trains a day: 75 starting from St

Right: King's Cross was designed by Lewis Cubitt and built in 1851-2. When it opened it was the biggest station in England.

Pancras; 10 from North of London and 65 from Waterloo. About a third of them will stop at Ashford. The Stratford-St Pancras section would see 84 international daily workings, 206 Kent Express commuter workings and 47 ecs workings.

CTRL distances

St Pancras-Stratford:	9.8km (6 miles)
Stratford-Ebbsfleet:	27.2km (17 miles)
Ebbsfleet-Ashford:	53km (33 miles)

St Pancras

St Pancras was, legend would have us believe, a 14-year-old convert to Christianity martyred by the Roman Emperor Diocletian in AD304. His cult was popularised in England by St Augustine. The parish church of St Pancras gave its name to both the borough (merged with Holborn in 1965 to give the Borough of Camden) and to the terminus of the Midland Railway, which bought the site in 1863.

Established by 'Railway King' George Hudson, the MR was one of the most active railways of the mid-19th century and found sharing a London terminus with the Great Northern Railway at King's Cross unsatisfactory. Between 1863 and 1867 to the design of W. H. Barlow a soaring 210m long train shed was built. But it is eclipsed in most people's memory by the wonderful Euston Road frontage of Gilbert Scott's Midland Hotel, a fantastic Gothic creation. 172m long, with a 82m clock tower and a 76m west tower, the

Left: The Midland Hotel, designed by Gilbert Scott, is one of Victorian London's greatest buildings.

Midland Hotel is one of London's great buildings dwarfing nearby King's Cross, which was built 1851-2.

St Pancras and the Midland Hotel survived the lean years when public subsidy was hardly enough for basic maintenance of rolling stock and lines. Indeed, the hotel closed in 1935 and became offices and BR even considered selling it off. Now it has a new lease of life for the new millennium — selected as the principal London terminus for the CTRL, this major project will see the extensive yards at the rear of St Pancras developed, the existing station will be refurbished. A competition has been launched for the development of the Chambers building the exterior of which, including the imposing Grade ! listed facade was recently renovated at a cost of £10 million.

The platform deck will be extended to over twice its current length to accommodate the longer trains and 13 platforms created in place of the present seven. This will accommodate the 400m long Eurostars and Kent express trains using the CTRL as well as services using the Midland main lines. The programme includes the construction of a new underground station for Thameslink 2000 cross-London regional rail service.

Left: Gilbert Scott's Midland Grand Hotel will provide a fitting view for international passengers arriving in London.

Ebbsfleet International

Ebbsfleet will be an M25 parkway, the centre of a planned new Thames-side residential and business community, together with a junction to the North Kent Railway enabling domestic trains to use the new railway.

Stratford International

Well positioned to serve Docklands and east London with its Underground and links to East Anglia, Stratford International has a bright future. With the option of bypassing St Pancras traffic from the north of England, Stratford will gain in importance. Eurostar trains should gain traffic too: the admittedly partial, Stratford Promoter Group have estimated a 15 per cent increase in traffic through Stratford.

Direct Connection to the West Coast Main Line

LCR's proposal is for a direct twin-track connection from the CTRL to the WCML filling the missing link to create an unbroken rail spine from the Channel Tunnel to Glasgow and by so doing setting up rail times and connections far in advance of existing ones. The connection should save up to 60min on Eurostar services from Glasgow, Manchester and Birmingham. It will use a link to the North London Line across the Railway Lands. The ECML will have a connection to the CTRL via St Pancras.

Location	Time to Paris	New Time	Saving
Glasgow	9hr 25min	8hr 25min	1hr
Edinburgh	8hr 25min	7hr 25min	1hr
Manchester	4hr 05min	3hr 05min	1hr
Crewe	5hr 25min	4hr 25min	1hr
Birmingham	5hr	4hr	1hr
Doncaster	5hr 30min	4hr 30min	1hr
Peterborough	4hr 30min	3hr 30min	1hr

This assumes approx journey times using existing rail routes via Kensington Olympia versus CTRL with WCML link in place

Location	Time to London	New Time	Saving
Dover	110min	70min	40min
Folkestone	95min	55min	40min
Ramsgate	115min	80min	35min
Margate	100min	80min	20min
Ashford	75min	40min	35min
Sittingbourne	65min	50min	15min
Medway Towns	45min	30min	15min
Gravesend	50min	20min	30min

This sets the present fastest peak period journey to London terminus against projected journey time to St Pancras.

Additional Destinations

The long undivided overhead luggage racks of Eurostar are ideal for ski storage - so a direct service is essential! It is hoped that the first Snow Specials will run in late 1997 (nine of the SNCF TMSTs are being modified to operate also at 1,500V dc for these services).

Regional (North of London) Services

The full impact of the new age of rail will become apparent through most of Britain once the regional Eurostar services have started. The regional trains are very similar to the intercapital service except that they are shorter by four carriages.

The sight of these new trains speeding through the countryside has reawakened the British public to the inherent advantages of rail travel. It could be that the folk memory of the Victorians' enthusiasm remained — for these services have been popular from the start. Our European cousins take their railways for granted — in the UK they remain in danger of being 'rationalised' out of existence. Many of the new owners of the fragmented privatised rail industry also run buses, which could provide an alternative if eco-unfriendly alternative in the event of the closure of railway lines. Who knows - these lines run directly into city centres and would provide ideal through routes for diesel buses! Regional Eurostar may provide the key to the long-term survival of rail in Britain by clearly demonstrating the advantages of modern high-speed train travel. Fortunately the marketing expertise of LCR will have an ideal environment in which to work its magic.

The regional Eurostars were ordered from TMSTG (see 'The Intercapital Service') on 18 December 1991. Seven sets were ordered, four new ones and three to be adapted from the original order for the intercapital Eurostars.

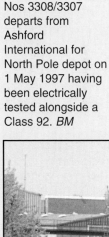

Below: Regional Eurostar set Nos 3308/3307 departs from Ashford International for North Pole depot on 1 May 1997 having been electrically tested alongside a Class 92. *BM*

Regional Eurostar trains have 14 carriages and two engines. There are 578 seats, 114 in First Class and 464 in Standard. There are two buffet cars, and it is planned to provide innovative on-board services.

It is planned that each morning, a Eurostar train will leave Glasgow for Paris, stopping at stations including Edinburgh, York and Peterborough. Another Eurostar will leave Manchester for Paris, stopping at Crewe and Milton Keynes among other places. Yet another will leave Birmingham New Street for Paris, stopping for instance at Coventry and Milton Keynes. Brussels will be served by changing trains at Lille. These Eurostars return from their destinations that same evening.

Typical journey times for regional Eurostar journeys:

Regional Station	Paris
Glasgow	9.25
Edinburgh	8.25
Newcastle	6.55
Darlington	6.25
York	5.55
Doncaster	5.30
Newark	5.05
Peterborough	4.30
Manchester Piccadilly	6.05
Stockport	5.55
Crewe	5.25
Stafford	5.05
Wolverhampton	5.25
Birmingham New Street	5.00
Birmingham International	4.50
Coventry	4.30
Rugby	4.10
Milton Keynes Central	3.45

These will be reduced with the opening of the CTRL.

Above: The Eurostar services beyond Waterloo International extend, via west and East Coast lines, to Manchester and Glasgow.

Eurostar

Chronology

8,000-7,000BC

The isthmus joining England to the continental land mass is finally eroded by the Atlantic and North Sea, and Britain becomes an island.

1802

Albert Mathieu, a French mining engineer, obtained an audience with Napoleon Bonaparte in order to submit a plan for a bored tube channel tunnel. Napoleon admired the scheme enough to tell the British Ambassador that it should be attempted by both countries together. Apart from public exhibitions of his plans in Paris, Mathieu was destined to see history override his visionary idea.

1803

Tessier de Mottray suggests a tunnel in the form of an immersed tube, ignoring the fact that the technology required for such a system did not exist.

1830s

Aime Thome de Gamond, a talented polymath, undertakes the first serious geological and hydrographic studies, including samples dredged from the seabed.

1856

de Gamond produces a scheme for a 34km tunnel in masonry, to take two rail tracks.

Overleaf: Eurostar waiting to depart from Waterloo International.

Below: Placement of a pre-cast concrete tunnel lining segment in the landward service tunnel.

1865

John Hawkshaw (later Sir John) working with a syndicate he had formed puts forward his proposal for a single-bore tunnel of 21ft diameter. William Low, an engineer working with him on the scheme, disagrees strongly and recommends the adoption of two single-track bores. Hawkshaw and his syndicate go on to form the English Channel Company. This marks the beginning of divergence on the British side with the eventual formation of rival companies with competing designs.

1866

de Gamond produces a modified version of his 1856 plan.

1867

Aime Thome de Gamond and William Low collaborate along with another English engineer named Brunlees. Their project is referred to an English parliamentary committee and a commission of French engineers.

1874

Creation of the French Channel Company.

Above: Further work in the scheme abandoned by the Labour government in 1975 sees a steel arch being positioned at the face of the 480m tunnel at the point from which contractors were to start work on the fixed link. *IAL*

Far right:
Construction of the cut-and-cover loop tunnel at the western extremity of the Folkestone site in February 1989.

1875

March William Low impresses Edward Watkin, (later Sir Edward), then chairman of the South Eastern Railway, who drums up funding for tunnel studies, and becomes chairman of the Anglo-French Submarine Railway Company.

2 August Bills passed in the British Parliament and the French Assembly. The British measure becomes The British Channel Tunnel Company (Limited) Act. This is followed by a protocol drafted by the Anglo-French commission.

1878

A 2,000yd exploratory tunnel bored by the French at Sangatte.

1881

Sir Edward Watkin launches a new SER-backed undertaking, the Submarine Continental Railway company, with Alexandre Lavalley. Nearly 4km of tunnel completed before digging is stopped by the British in 1882.

1882

23 February Formation of the Channel Tunnel Defence Committee, set up by the War Office. Beginnings of military objections to the Tunnel. Both Hawkshaw's and Watkin's Bills fail to get through Parliament, and the government calls a halt to further work.

18 March The French, dismayed at the British decision, stop work at Sangatte.

1883

Watkin finally forced to close his works at Shakespeare Cliff.

1886

Watkin buys out the rival Hawkshaw company, and forms the new Channel Tunnel Company, under which name it will continue for the next 90 years.

1890

5 June Watkin addresses Parliament in his final attempt to restart work. He is outvoted.

1904

Albert Satiaux of the French Nord Railway, and Sir Francis Fox make new technical studies of the Tunnel. They agree that the de Gamond/Low principle of twin single-line tunnels is correct.

1906

A new Channel Tunnel Bill is introduced in Parliament, but once again is defeated and withdrawn by its sponsors in 1907.

1913

11 June A new Channel Tunnel parliamentary committee is formed. Arthur Fell (later Sir) was chairman.

5 August Fell sees the Prime Minister Asquith, who characteristically hedges and then continues the policy of rejection.

23 September The Franco-British Travel Union holds a congress at which Percy Tempest shows a collection of Tunnel drawings. Asquith refers the matter to the traditionally hostile Admiralty and War Office, who are to report to the Committee of Imperial Defence.

1914

15 July The Committee of Imperial Defence reports against the Channel Tunnel.

1915-19

Fell and his colleagues put five different parliamentary motions for debate, to no avail. Fell is told that the matter will not be considered whilst the war is on.

1919-22

No fewer than 19 unsuccessful attempts are made to get Parliament to reconsider the whole question.

1922

Fell hands over the chairmanship of the Channel Tunnel Parliamentary Committee to Sir William Bull, who continues to fight valiantly and tirelessly for the Tunnel until his death in 1931.

1924

The first Labour Government takes office and Prime Minister Ramsay Macdonald, having been

pursued and pressured by Bull, convenes a meeting between himself and four former Prime Ministers — Asquith, Lloyd George, Balfour and Baldwin. Each man reaffirms his opposition to the Tunnel, and Macdonald, pleased with this support for a do-nothing policy, declares in the House of Commons that the question of a Channel Tunnel is in need of reappraisal, and promptly refers the matter once again to the Imperial Defence Committee! Within three weeks the IDC running true to form restates its opposition to the Tunnel.

July Winston Churchill enters the debate — writing articles and speaking in the House of Commons he attacks the Establishment for its lack of vision, criticising the antiquated attitudes that colour their decisions. Despite his acid wit, nothing happens.

1925

November Prime Minister Baldwin refuses to reopen the debate.

1926

November Again Baldwin refuses to budge from his position.

1927

May Baldwin has "Nothing to add."

1928

May Baldwin: "The time is unripe."

1929

January Sir William Bull is finally successful in obtaining a debate in the Commons, in which Baldwin gives way and agrees to another Royal Commission.

February The Royal Commission sits, and delegates the detailed technical work of the study to a sub-contractor, with the brief to consider a tunnel, and any other new form of cross-Channel communications. This widening of the brief opens the door to alternative schemes of dubious worth and relevance, including a massive jetty stretching across the Channel from Dover to Calais, a bridge, immersed tubes and train ferries (which the two railway companies immediately focused on). A certain William Collard proposes a tunnel, but also a high-speed rail link from London to Paris which could make the journey in 2hr 45min — a

proposal similar to the one put forward and accepted by the two governments in 1973!

1930

28 February The report finally emerges, and is on the whole encouraging and in favour of the Tunnel.

29 May Prime Minister Macdonald seeks to delay and consults the IDC again. The military reaffirm their objection to the Tunnel.

30 June Supporters of the Tunnel force a debate in the Commons. Macdonald makes a lengthy speech in opposition. Results of the voting: For: 172, Against: 179. The two train companies turn seriously to train-ferries.

1932

Inauguration of train-ferry services btween Dover and Dunkirk. (Three train-ferries built.)

1937

Baron Emile D'Erlanger retires as chairman of the Channel Tunnel Company, being replaced by Sir Herbert Walker, who leaves his post of General Manager of Southern Railways to assume his new position.

1939

November With the British Expeditionary Force in France, the French Chamber of Deputies demand that the Channel Tunnel should be built! But the war effectively stalls the whole process again, with perhaps the only useful progression being the evolution of air power — thus obviating the military objections to the Tunnel.

1947

17 March Christopher Shawcross, a young Labour MP, takes the lead in reviving the Channel Tunnel Parliamentary Group (CTPG).

July The CTPG produces a report estimating the cost of the Tunnel at £65.5 million. Military objections are ridiculed in the new age of rockets and nuclear weapons.

1948

January The Labour Government nationalises the railway companies. (The French railways were nationalised in 1937.)

1955

Harold Macmillan, then Minister of Defence, says in the Commons that the Tunnel poses scarcely any military risk. Following a study SHAPE — Supreme Headquarters Allied Powers Europe — announce that the West's defences would be greatly strengthened by a tunnel underneath the Channel connecting the UK to the Continent.

1957

March Technical Studies Inc — a corporation made up of both Americans and Europeans is launched in America by Tunnel sympathisers to finance technical investigations, one of which is begun on the feasibility of the Tunnel.

6 July Four companies — the two British and French Channel Tunnel Companies, the Suez Canal Company and Technical Studies Incorporated form the Channel Tunnel Study Group to co-operate on all aspects of the Tunnel.

1959

February The British Channel Tunnel Company Parliamentary Committee (BCTCPC) hires a consulting engineers company called Colquhoun to carry out a massive in depth study of feasibility for the Tunnel.

April The report is released to the Channel Tunnel Study Group, including information on the geological structure of the seabed. The group then go on to commission a massive definitive report on all other technical and financial aspects of the project.

1960

March The reports and studies gathered together by the Channel Tunnel Study Group and given to the BCTCPC are regarded as the fundamental plan of the Tunnel. The basis of the scheme is accepted by the government between 1966 and 1974, and then suddenly dropped in 1975. (It is also

accepted as the parent of the 1985 plan.) These delays represent the lack of political will and drive — more evident on the British side. Despite the formidable array of experts and coming up with detailed plans including all aspects of the Tunnel and the rail links on either side of it have the BCTCPC had an anti-European government to contend with.

1966

8 July Premiers Wilson and Pompidou announce the intention of building the Tunnel.

28 October Barbara Castle and her French counterpart M Pisani confirm the commitment to build the Tunnel, and invite all interested parties to submit plans and designs.

1968

Transport Act of Parliament includes a provision for setting up a Channel Tunnel Planning Council

23 October New Transport Minister Richard Marsh and his French counterpart M Chamant announce they have completed their consideration of all the proposals submitted.

11 November Marsh declares in the Commons that the chosen design will be announced in early 1969, but a General Election intrudes.

1970

15 July New Transport Minister John Peyton announces that a new Channel Tunnel Company would construct the British half of the project. The old company, which dated back to 1887, would be renamed Channel Tunnel Investments Ltd, and become a founder shareholder of the new company. On the French side a new construcion company is also formed — the Société Française du Tunnel Sous la Manche.

1972

20 October The two governments sign parallel agreements with the new companies, known as Agreement Number 1, providing for the work to be carried out by July 1975. But British Rail's four alternative high-speed routes to Folkestone cause a furore and, at £450+ million, rival the cost of the British input to the Chunnel.

1973

September The government announces a high quality rail link between the Tunnel and London is essential to the success of the project. (It would have run from a White City passenger terminal to a Tunnel portal at Folkestone. The London end was illogical, nowhere near an

Right: Route learning saloon No 931001 passes Wandsworth Road arcing well en route from Clapham Yard to Dover on 20 September 1993. *Chris Wilson*

Underground station, and there were many objections.)

1975

January The Labour Government abandons the project. The single most important reason is the disruption of the progress of the Channel Tunnel Bill through Parliament, caused by two General Elections. Also there is an anti-tunnel groundswell. The two Tunnel companies suggested a new timetable, with a new Bill in the autumn of 1975, and a commitment to start work by the end of 1976. When there are further delays and prevarication on the part of the government, pushed on by its anti-Europe stance, the two Tunnel companies take legal advice, convinced that the government is backing out. And they are reverting to those peculiarly xenophobic attitudes manifested earlier on time and time again in the history of the Tunnel's development. One important decision is made: no long-term developments will take place in Kent in the likely area of a Tunnel portal.

1976

January The project with the first Channel Tunnel founders and dies.

1981

11 September France and the UK announce the launch of studies of a fixed link under the Channel. Various proposals are studied including bridges linking in to a central island, road transport only tunnels, and composite ideas.

1986

20 January Maragret Thatcher and François Mitterrand announce that they have chosen the Eurotunnel project: a dual rail tunnel for trains and shuttles carrying motor vehicles.

1987

January TMSTG is formed (TransManche Super Train Group) to bid for the trains to be used in the Tunnel. A joint venture between three national consortia.
February The Channel Tunnel receives the Royal Assent.
Waterloo station chosen as the London international rail passenger terminal.
29 July Thatcher and Mitterrand exchange ratification of the Canterbury treaty.
July King's Cross chosen for the second London international passenger terminal.

Left: The late Roy Castle is seen with Eurostar staff at the naming of a Class 47 locomotive after him. The locomotive had just hauled a nationwide special around Britain to promote cancer awareness.

August DoT publishes Kent Impact Study, which states extra rail capacity is needed.

15 December Channel Tunnel construction begins.

1988

BR, SNCF and SNCB form IPG — the International Project Group — to co-ordinate the procurement of trains for the Tunnel.

July Protest groups emerge across Kent and south London.

November BR Board invites six private companies to design, build, finance and operate the rail link to the Tunnel.

1989

January King's Cross chosen as second terminal site.

18 December The three railway networks sign a contract for an initial 30 Eurostar trainsets with a consortium of builders led by GEC-Alsthom.

This order is later supplemented by purchase of additional train units to serve NoL and this set the number of trains at 31 'Three Capitals' and seven NoL.

1990

October Detailed plans of Waterloo International are approved by Secretary of State for Environment.

30 October At 19.30 the two ends of the service tunnel meet in mid-channel.

1 December Official breakthrough ceremony.

1991

28 June The tunnel boring is completed.

1992

June EPS awards GEC/Metro-Cammell the £120 million contract to build the Nightstar trains.

Below: Prototype Eurostar PS-1 passes through Kensington Olympia from North Pole to Dollands Moor. The unit is hauled by Class 73 Nos 73118/30.
Chris Wilson

1993

January The Eurostar PS-1 (short-set)— the first of a new generation of trains — leaves the production line for testing.

17 May Waterloo International Terminal is formally handed over to Sir Bob Reid by contractors John Brown on time.

20 June The first Eurostar PS-1 travels through the Tunnel pulled by a diesel loco.

1 July Trials with the pre-production PS-2.

6 July PS-2 runs at 305km/hr on new TGV Nord line.

24 September First French production train delivered to SNCF (F1).

October Work begins at Ashford International.

31 October First production train produced in England delivered to SNCB (UK1).

11 November British Government announces competition for private sector interest in construction of CTRL in UK.

1994

22 February First train tested in Belgium to ensure smooth transition from 3,000V dc of the

Above: In December 1989 French Channel Tunnel construction workers celebrate the arrival of a Japanese-built running tunnel boring machine (TBM) from Sangatte to the Bessingue portal on the Coquelles Terminal site near Calais. *Eurotunnel*

Left: Her Majesty Queen Elizabeth II at the inauguration of Eurostar at Waterloo International.

Above: Completed power car No 3014 is pictured in the GEC-Alsthom works at Washwood Heath on 25 May 1994 prior to delivery. *BM*

conventional rail lines to the high-speed lines' 25,000V ac.

March Changeover test from BR's 750V network to the Tunnel's 25,000V

13 April Eurostar high-speed test run between Paris and Arras.

6 May Inauguration of the Tunnel by Queen Elizabeth and President Mitterrand.

24 May Calais-Fréthun opens to public service

1 June First automotive train from Britain to Europe loaded with Rovers bound for Arluno, Italy.

July Channel Tunnel opens for freight services.

2 August Authority is received from the InterGovernmental Commission (IGC) for a reduced passenger-carrying test service for the Shuttle, and for Eurostar passenger trains.

17 August First introductory journey with personnel from the three companies on board Eurostar trains.

20 October Record set from London to Paris — 2hr 48min.

November Royal Institute of British Architects choose Waterloo International as Building of the Year.

13 November Charles de Gaulle station opens to traffic,

14 November First Eurostar commercial services begin from London at 10.13 to Paris and 10.23 to Brussels with the opening of Waterloo International.

24 November Hybrid Bill seeking to gain parliamentary approval for the CTRL introduced into House of Commons.

21 December Conventional freight starts to transit through the Tunnel in the form of Railfreight Distribution's first trainload of steel slabs from Tinsley bound for Sweden.

22 December Le Shuttle opens its public services.

1995

16 January CTRL Bill gets second reading

21 January Boulogne Maritime and Calais Maritime stations close because of Eurostar competition. On 1 April an experimental service reopens (or is this an April Fool's Day joke?).

23 January Eurostars start calling at Calais-Fréthun.

13-18 April 56,000 people use Eurostar over the Easter holidays with a day's record of 11,000 on Easter Monday.

23 May One millionth passenger travels by Eurostar.

28 June First NoL short-formation Eurostar delivered by Metro-Cammell (part of the GEC-Alsthom group).

27 July Railtrack approves updating scheme to give Eurostar access to ECML.

31 August Two millionth passenger travels by Eurostar.

6 September Prince Michael of Kent opens new domestic station at Ashford.

3 October Ceremony to mark the start of track-laying of Belgian high-speed line.

23 December Three millionth passenger travels by Eurostar.

1996

8 January Start of service from Ashford International station.

28 February Formal opening of Ashford International by HRH Duke of Kent.

29 February London & Continental Railways announced as the company chosen to construct the Channel Tunnel Rail Link in UK.

1 April Four millionth passenger travels on Eurostar.

1 June LCR takes over.

1 October EPS renamed Eurostar (UK) Ltd

18 November Fire in one tunnel bore leads to temporary cessation of services.

18 December Royal Assent granted for the construction of the British high-speed line.

29 December Eight millionth passenger carried.

1997

15 March Nine millionth passenger carried.

28 April Launch of Premium First.

7 May Ten millionth passenger carried.

1 June Full services resume after Channel Tunnel fire.

12 July Eleven millionth passenger carried.

Below: A contrast in front ends. A Eurostar TMST and an SNCF TGV run alongside through the French countryside.

Appendix 2

Technical Specification

Design

A tri-national team of designers was involved in Eurostar design. Roger Tallon, the French prize-winning designer renowned for his contribution to SNCF's Corail and the TGV Atlantique was in charge of the external livery and the carriages; Belgian Jacques Tillman worked on other parts of the train's interior. Brit Roger Jones was responsible for rounding the nose of the power car and the inside design of the driver's cab and the bars. Pierre Balmain designed the uniforms for the staff and the Eurostar logo reflected all the qualities of the train: stars for the future, the three lines of the three European partners.

Train Formation

The Three Capitals trains are comprised of 18 coaches (or trailer vehicles) formed of two identical nine-car 'half-sets' marshalled back-to-back with a power car at each end making a total train formation of 20 vehicles, 394 m (1,292 ft) in length. The trailer vehicles are designated 'R' for 'remorque' and the power cars 'M' for 'motrice'. Within the formation, the vehicles are also individually assigned numbers as shown below.

Bogies

Unlike conventional coaching stock, the trailer vehicles within the half-set are 'articulated' and share a common two-axled bogie between intermediate vehicle ends. This has the effect of reducing the number of wheelsets in contact with the rail and also helps improve ride quality. As a result, in order to reduce the load on the axles and to remain within the structural loading gauge on corners, the vehicles are much shorter than conventional coaching stock. As uncoupling vehicles within the half-set is not possible by this arrangement, the vehicles remain as a fixed formation and any maintenance is undertaken on a half-set basis rather than as individual vehicles.

The end trailer vehicles within each half-set (ie R1, R9, R10 and R18) have one non-articulated two-axled bogie at the outer end. These vehicles are slightly longer as they are supported by an equivalent of three axles rather than two. On the R1 and R18 vehicles the end bogies are powered (similar to TGV Sud-Est trains) with electrical traction power equipment located directly above.

Each power car has two non-articulated two-axled powered bogies making a total of 12 powered axles per train (six at each end). Each

Overleaf: No 3013 in the GEC-Alsthom yard at Washwood Heath. *BM*

Right: View of a Eurostar's bogie.

M1 + R1 + R2 + R3 + R4 + R5 + R6 + R7 + R8 + R9 + R10 + R11 + R12 + R13 + R14 + R15 + R16 + R17 + R18 + M2

half-set   half-set

power car bogie has two retractable shoes on each side which are used to collect current when operating over the British third-rail system. The traction motors which provide power to the wheels are suspended from the vehicle body to reduce the 'unsprung mass' in order to minimise track damage at high speed.

The length of the bogie wheelbases is 3,000mm and the distance between bogie centres is 14m and 18.7m for power car and intermediate trailer vehicles respectively.

Wheelsets

All bogies have two wheelsets which consist of a hollow steel axle to reduce weight and to permit quicker maintenance inspection, two steel monobloc wheels (ie one piece), four solid steel brake discs on non-powered bogies and a final drive transmission housing on powered bogies. The width between the tracks is standard across all three countries at 1,435 mm (4ft 8½in). The wheel diameter is 920mm when new, reducing to 850mm before replacement is necessary.

To reduce track damage at high speeds the vehicles are designed to have a maximum axle load of 17 tonnes in order to satisfy the requirements for the SNCF high-speed line.

Weight

An entire train formation ranges in weight from 752.4 tonnes when empty, to 816.0 tonnes when fully laden.

Vehicle Structure

All vehicles are assembled using a steel 'monocoque' bodyshell (ie no chassis). The vehicle nose of the power car is manufactured using glass reinforced plastic (GRP) to obtain the aesthetic contours and aerodynamic performance. The nose is tapered to remain within the structural loading gauge when negotiating corners. In the event of an accident, risk of injury to the driver is minimised by a steel safety cage around the driving position with an energy absorption ('crumple') zone, approximately 1m³ in size, at the front.

The structural loading gauge within Britain is much smaller than the standard UIC gauge and the structure was therefore redesigned, reducing the overall width from 2,900mm to 2,814mm

and lowering the roof by some 330mm. Other modifications to minimise protrusion of vehicle suspension damper mountings and pantograph supports were also necessary.

Suspension

All vehicle bodyshells have two stages of suspension:

a) Primary suspension — between wheelsets and the bogie frame. Each wheelset is mounted on two pivoting arms attached to each side of the bogie frame. These are supported by a coil spring and hydraulic damper on each arm.

b) Secondary suspension — between the bogie frame and the vehicle bodyshell. On the trailer bogies this takes the form of an air bag. Level sensors automatically adjust the pressure within the bag to accommodate different passenger loadings. On the power car bogies, coil and

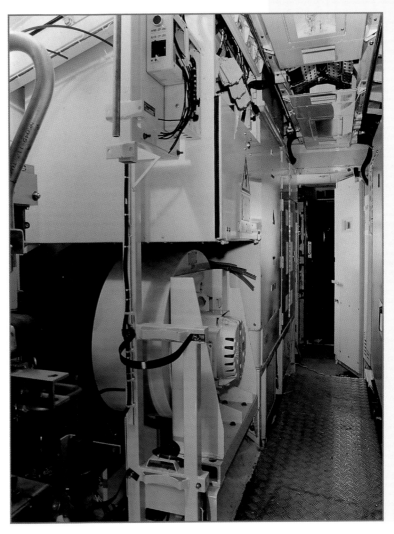

Below: The interior of one of the TMST power cars.

147

Eurostar

Right: The seating plan of the first nine coaches of a Eurostar train; there are only two smoking compartments, coach 12 (first class) and coach 14 (standard class).

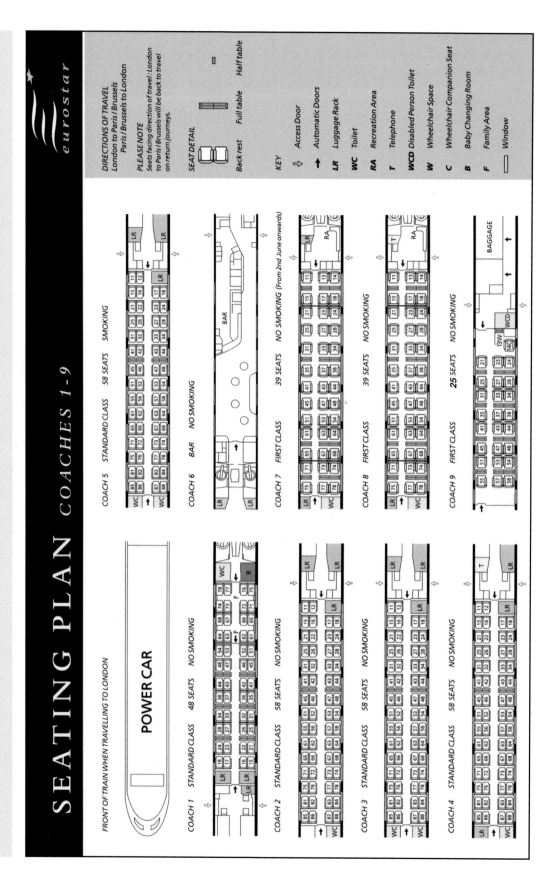

elastomer springs, and hydraulic dampers are utilised as the weight of the vehicle remains virtually constant. These provide good stability to the vehicle, ensuring minimum deviation of the pantograph when in contact with the overhead wire when negotiating corners at high speed.

In addition, movement between articulated vehicle bodyshells is restricted by the use of four hydraulic dampers located between vehicle corners in line with the train (ie. longitudinally) and a single hydraulic damper mounted horizontally across the width of the vehicles (ie laterally). This effectively forms a 'semi-rigid snake' of vehicles which is supported on a cushion of air, by the relatively soft secondary suspension. This acts as a very effective form of insulation between track noise and the passenger environment and gives the vehicles their superior ride quality characteristics. The maximum longitudinal movement is limited to about 100mm within each half-set.

Hydraulic yaw dampers fitted between the vehicle bodies and bogie frame give the bogies good stability at high speed. Anti-roll bars fitted between the bogies and vehicle body on the trailers enable the vehicles to have a soft ride but are able to remain within the tight structural loading gauge requirements of Britain.

The suspension system on Eurostar is particularly noted for its adaptability under the contrasting track conditions of the purpose-built French high-speed line and the curved suburban lines of southern England. The smoothness of the ride often gives the impression that the train is travelling much slower than it actually is!

The suspension system's low noise transfer characteristics and sealed gangways dramatically reduce the rather harsh environment often found between conventional coaching stock vehicles. This is pleasantly received by customers, especially children, who are often intimidated by the passage from one vehicle to another on traditional vehicles.

Vehicle Interior

Close attention has been paid to the comfort of the passenger in both the interior design of the vehicles and on-train facilities offered. The vehicles boast pleasant spacious accommodation coupled with both durability and versatility for the future.

The Three Capitals vehicles are equipped as shown in the table below.

This gives a total train capacity of 766 seats of which 206 seats are First Class and 560 are Standard Class. An additional 52 fold-down seats are provided in the vehicle vestibules.

The catering equipment includes two microwave ovens, two convection ovens and refrigerated cabinets.

Performance

The maximum commercial speed of Eurostar is 300km/hr (186mph) when operating on the specially constructed high-speed lines in France, and soon, when complete, in Belgium.

Until the Channel Tunnel Rail Link (CTRL) is completed, the speed is limited to a maximum of 160km/hr (100mph) south of

Vehicle	Class	Smoking	Seats	Toilets	Additional Facilities
R1/R18	2nd	No	48	1	Nursery/Family Area/ Baby Changing Facility
R2/R17	2nd	No	58	1	Train Manager's Office
R3/R16	2nd	No	58	2	
R4/R15	2nd	No	58	1	Telephone
R5/R14	2nd	Yes	58	2	
R6/R13	Buffet	No	-	-	Bar and Catering Area
R7/R12	1st	Yes	39	1	Relaxation Area
R8/R11	1st	No	39	1	Telephone
R9/R10	1st	No	25	-	Disabled Persons' Area and Toilet Luggage Compartment

London. This speed limit is also imposed when travelling through the Channel Tunnel.

Tests have been conducted in France, under special conditions, which enabled a TGV Atlantique train formation to set a new rail world speed record on 18 May 1990 of 515.3km/hr (320mph). To date, no attempts have been made better this with the higher powered Eurostar trains. However, with the same degree of preparation, similar record attempts could be made.

Braking System

There are two types of braking system used on Eurostar. These are:

a) Friction braking system. On each non-powered bogie wheelset two sintered metal brake pads are used to grip each of the four steel discs mounted along the length of the axle. On powered bogies brake shoes are pressed against the tread of the wheels, to assist in cleaning, and therefore help preventing the wheels from slipping. The braking system is pneumatically operated with air delivered from the power cars along the length of the train by means of two pipes. One pipe provides an air supply to all the vehicle pneumatic systems and is used to apply the brakes. The other pipe provides a control signal dependent upon the air pressure within the pipe to determine braking effort required. Electrical control signals (known as EP Assist) are also sent down the length of the train and operate air pressure control valves on each vehicle locally. These help speed up the rate at which the air pressure control signal is propagated down the length of the pipe ensuring all vehicles are applying the same braking force to the wheels as demanded from the driving cab. The kinetic energy of the train is dissipated as heat and brake disc temperatures of over 500°C have been measured.

b) 'Rheostatic' braking system. When travelling above 40km/hr (25mph), to reduce wear of the brake pads and shoes, the electric motors used to power the train are used in reverse as electric generators. A resistive load, known as a rheostat, is connected to the motor which causes it to decelerate. The effect of this is transmitted back through the transmission resulting in a braking effect to the wheels. The kinetic energy of the train is converted into electrical energy by the traction motors and then into heat within the rheostatic braking stacks mounted within both the power car and ends of vehicles R1 and R18. The maximum energy converted by all six rheostatic braking stacks is in the order of 9.8MW.

Where possible the power car will try to take as much advantage of the rheostatic braking system as possible. However, when the braking

Below: Top view of a power car with the roof covers unmounted. *GEC-Alsthom*

demand exceeds the rating of the rheostatic brake a sophisticated computer is used to 'blend' the amount of braking effort provided by the two systems working in parallel with each other. The power car friction brakes are used only below 40km/hr and in an emergency

In the event of an emergency, only the friction braking system is used to apply the brakes.

When travelling at a speed of 300km/hr the train is able to stop within a maximum distance of 3.5km (2.2 miles) but in good adhesion conditions this is more typically 3.0 km (1.9 miles). With a maximum deceleration force of 965kN (13%g) this brings the train to rest within a time of about 65 seconds.

On average, the brake pads for the disc brakes must be renewed every 9 months.

Electrical Power System

In order to operate over the infrastructure of three countries, Eurostar needs to be compatible with three different sources of electrical power supply. These are:

a) 25kV 50Hz ac supplied from overhead wires (catenary) when operating in France, within the Channel Tunnel and when inside North Pole International Depot in northwest London.

b) 3kV dc supplied from overhead catenary when operating in Belgium.

c) 750V dc supplied by a third rail adjacent to the running lines when operating over the railways of southern Britain.

The maximum traction power demand by the train is 12.24MW (16,400 bhp). As the train is significantly longer than French TGVs, the installed power is the highest ever installed on a high speed train. By comparison, this is significantly greater than the 6MW TGV Sud-Est and 8.8MW TGV Réseau trains.

Due to power supply restrictions in Belgium and Britain (under third-rail operation) the train is limited to 5.7MW and 5.1MW in these countries respectively. This however does not impact on the train's performance as the maximum permissible speed on these lines is the limiting factor.

As there are three different power supply voltages, each Eurostar power car is fitted with three forms of current collection device:

a) A 25kV pantograph mounted on the vehicle roof.

b) A 3kV pantograph mounted adjacent to it.

c) 750V retractable current pick-up shoes mounted on both bogies.

When travelling from London, the changeover from 750V to 25kV is performed on the move at Dollands Moor, Kent. After selection of 'Eurotunnel mode' by the driver, the shoegear is retracted on both power cars, followed by the raising of the 25kV pantographs upwards until they come into contact with the overhead wire. If the train is travelling to Brussels a second voltage changeover must be performed at the Belgian border. In this instance both 25kV pantographs are retracted and the 3kV pantographs are extended. On the return journey the reverse of these processes is conducted.

It is necessary to have two types of pantograph as they have different widths, aerodynamic performance and current carrying capacity. However, the 3kV pantograph may be used to replace the 25kV pantograph in an emergency.

The electric power equipment, which is used to provide power to the electric motors, operates from a 1,900V dc supply source known as the link voltage. The input voltage to the train from all three infrastructure power systems must therefore be converted to a common dc supply, to avoid the need for three different types of traction system. This is performed by a large electrical cubicle called the common bloc, located centrally within the power car.

When operating from a 25kV ac supply the current is passed via a large transformer to two rectifier banks located within the common bloc. Each rectifier bank is used to convert the stepped down ac voltage on the secondary windings to a nominal 1,900V dc using a combination of high power diode and thyristor semi-conductors. The current is then passed through two stages of electrical filter to produce a smooth output. The transformer tank is made of aluminium to reduce vehicle weight.

When operating from a 3kV dc supply the current is passed via electrical filters to an electrical device known as a chopper, located within the common bloc. This switches the current passing through it on and off very quickly, using gate turn-off thyristor (GTO) power semi-conductors, which has the effect of reducing the average output voltage to 1,900V dc. The output voltage is then smoothed using an electrical filter.

When operating from a 750V dc supply the current is passed directly to the two-stage electrical filter. As the traction equipment will still function with a link voltage as low as 440V dc there is no requirement to convert the input supply. At this voltage level there is still enough power capability to maintain the journey times and maximum speed in southeast England.

All power circuits within the common bloc are completely duplicated for reliability purposes.

The transformer and electrical filter components are cooled using a high temperature non-flammable silicone-based oil system. The power semi-conductors are cooled by circulating a synthetic organic ester through heatsinks in the modules.

The two 1,900V dc links located within the common bloc are connected by an assembly of high power switches to three motor bloc electrical cubicles and two separate 'Train Auxiliary Choppers'. The configurations of the switches are automatically altered should a defect with one item of equipment occur, in order to maximise the redundancy obtained through having several pieces of equipment capable of performing the same operation.

Each motor bloc is used to provide power to two traction motors which deliver the driving force to one of the three powered bogies. Two motor blocs are located within the power car and one is located within the R1/R18 vehicle. The motor bloc contains two 'inverters' which convert the link voltage to a variable frequency and variable voltage ac supply for each of the two motors. This is performed by using GTOs which switch the link voltage on and off very quickly for controlled durations to replicate three-phase ac output voltage waveforms. As the train accelerates the GTO on/off patterns are changed to increase the frequency of the supply and hence the speed of the motor. The high power resistors used for rheostatic braking are located next to the motor blocs. In addition the motor blocs can derive their own supply from their own dedicated batteries via a link pre-charger which enables rheostatic braking to be achieved in the absence of an external vehicle power supply. Each motor bloc also contains a 'Bloc Auxiliary Chopper' (BAC) to feed its own cooling pumps and fans.

Eurostar employs the use of 12 'asynchronous' three-phase ac traction motors which offer excellent torque and speed characteristics. This is the first time a motor of the type has been used on a high-speed train akin to the TGV design. TGV Sud-Est trains use 12 dc motors whereas TGV Atlantique trains utilise eight synchronous ac machines. The Eurostar asynchronous motor design is very efficient and can deliver 1,020kW from a package less than 1m³. The absence of carbon to copper contact within the motor delivers high reliability and maintenance savings. The output from the motor is delivered to the axle via a speed reduction gear box mounted on the end of the motor, driveshaft and transmission housing located on the axle.

With only six motors in operation the train would still be able to negotiate a gradient of 25% (1 in 4). In poor adhesion conditions the train is able to direct sand underneath the driving wheels to increase grip.

Electrical Supply To The Trailers

The two Train Auxiliary Choppers (TACs), located within the common bloc, provide power to all the trailer vehicles within the train through the use of intervehicle cabling. The link voltage is stepped-down using a chopper to 530V dc. The TACs are also used to supply auxiliary power to the common blocs and other auxiliary equipment within the traction system (eg battery chargers and air compressors).

Normally the trailers are fed from both ends of the train, but in the event of equipment failure all vehicles will still function correctly with only two out of four TACs in operation, but air-conditioning performance may be limited.

The 530V dc supplies known as the train supply are used to power the trailer vehicle heating systems. On vehicles R5, R8, R11 and R14 the train supply is connected to a 250 kVA inverter. This is used to convert the dc into a 380V ac three-phase supply. This is used to power the vehicle air-conditioning and other electrical systems. The 380V ac supply is connected through intervehicle jumpers to all vehicles within the half-set.

72V batteries for the trailer vehicles are located within vehicles R3, R7, R12 and R16.

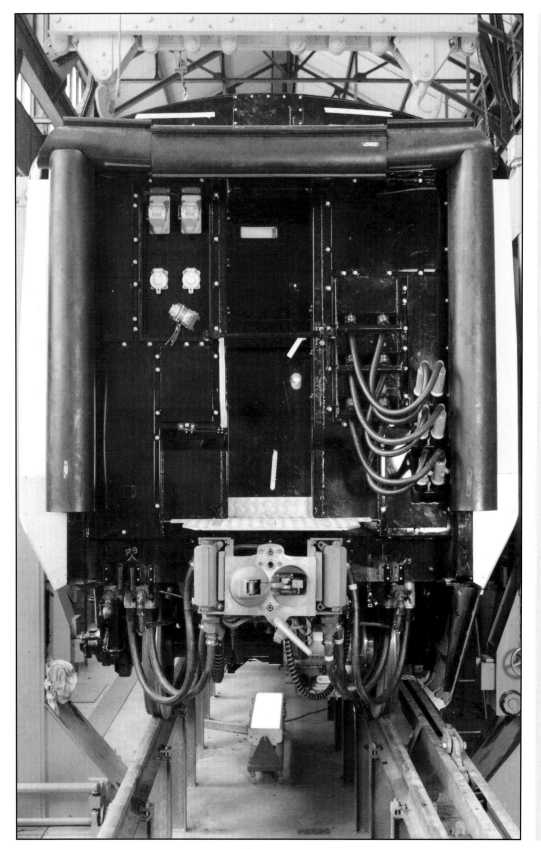

Left: The blunt end of one of the TMST power cars showing the connections that are made with the first of the coaches in each half-set.

Above: The driver's cab and controls. *GEC-Alsthom*

These are used to provide power to essential vehicle loads in the event of a power supply failure (eg emergency lighting, communications equipment, etc). Each battery has its own 30kW battery charger supplied from the 530V dc supply.

Lighting

Eurostar trailer vehicles have both fluorescent and low energy halogen lighting. Each seat has an individual switchable reading light and First Class vehicles have a table lamp.

Communication Systems

Eurostar has a sophisticated computer-controlled communication system which permits voice communication between the Driving Cab, Train Manager's Office, Police and Customs Office and vestibule handsets. In addition, it is also possible for communication to be established with numerous signalling control centres in each of the three countries

and with Eurotunnel Control itself using the International Train Radio (ITR).

Four telephones are available for passenger use which operate in all countries except when the train is in the Channel Tunnel.

Water System

Water for the toilets and wash basins is contained within a tank located under each trailer vehicle. Used water and effluent is treated and stored in retention tanks and removed at the end of the day's service.

Signalling System

Eurostar is equipped with five different signalling systems for operation over the infrastructure of the three countries:

a) TVM430 — for operation on the French high speed line and within the Channel Tunnel.

This is an in-cab signalling system which gives the driver information regarding the maximum permissible speed. There are no lineside signals as with conventional signalling systems owing to the speed of the train and the distance required to stop. If the driver fails to slow down when required, an automatic brake application will be made until the desired speed is attained.

b) KVB — for operation on the 'classical' infrastructure in France. The train activates transponders in the track which indicate the permitted speed to the driver.

c) TBL — for operation in Belgium. This is the Belgian equivalent of KVB.

d) 'Crocodile' (BRS) — for operation in France and Belgium. This system is so named because the transducers on the track, with which the receivers on the train make physical contact, are zigzag shaped and hence look like the ridge down a crocodile's back. With this system the driver is given an indication as to the status of the next signal he is about to approach.

e) AWS — for operation in Great Britain. This system employs the use of permanent and electro-magnets located between the tracks. A receiver mounted on the train passing over the magnets informs the driver of the train of the status of the next lineside signal he will encounter.

Switching between different signalling systems is done automatically by the train.

Driving Cab

The Eurostar driving cab is one of the most technologically advanced in the world. It boasts a once unique central driving position, single windscreen, computer fault diagnostic panel, pre-selection 'cruise' speed control, air-conditioning and soundproofing along with all the controls, visual and audio indicators necessary for operation across the three railways and within the Channel Tunnel. Its design was agreed between the three railways through both consultation and negotiation to achieve the best ergonomic solution.

The speedometer displays the train speed in mph in Britain and km/hr elsewhere.

Passenger Information Displays

Liquid Crystal Displays (LCDs) mounted on the exterior of the trailer vehicles adjacent to the doors inform the passengers on the platform of the coach number and the train destination. Similar displays are also provided inside the train above the vestibule doors.

Doors And Steps

Each trailer vehicle has two passenger doors, one on each side of the vehicle. The doors are

Left: Eurostar under construction in GEC-Alsthom works at Washwood Heath on 25 May 1994.
BM

Right: The first coach in each half-set provides 24 Standard Class seats along with additional space for control equipment.

Right: The first coach in each half-set provides 24 Standard Class seats along with additional space for control equipment.

electro-pneumatically operated and closed under control of the Train Manager using a console in the train vestibules. The doors can only be unlocked by the driver.

Platform heights vary between each of the three countries and within the Channel Tunnel:
- 550mm (21.6in) above rails in France
- 915mm (36in) in Great Britain
- 760mm (30in) in Belgium

Steps automatically deploy when the doors are opened to aid access to lower platforms. The steps retract when the doors are closed prior to train departure. Each door has an upper and lower step. The upper step is deployed in all countries and an additional second lower step is only deployed on the Continent and within the Channel Tunnel.

Fire Precautions

All electrical equipment located within the power car and the R1/R18 trailers is protected by a sophisticated fire detection and extinguisher system. Should a fire be detected, the equipment within that area will be shut down, a fire alarm will sound and after 20 seconds a Halon extinguishant will be released. The fresh air intake ducts to the air-conditioning systems are also sealed off to prevent ingress of smoke into the passenger areas.

For seated areas standard hand-held fire extinguishers are provided.

If a fire is detected within the Channel Tunnel, the driver is instructed to continue with the journey and not to stop. On emerging from the tunnel, the train will be brought to a stand where it will be met by a fire crew who will extinguish the fire as necessary.

All equipment fitted to the train is designed with this requirement in mind. On entrance to the Channel Tunnel additional yellow fire doors close between vehicles. Passage from vehicle to vehicle is still possible but these doors offer 30 minutes resistance to the spread of fire.

All materials used in the construction of Eurostar have been specially chosen for their excellent fire, smoke and fume resistance properties and comply with many of the stringent international standards (eg NFF 16101) often specified for underground railways/metros.

The vehicle floors and bulkheads between the electrical equipment also offer 30 minutes' protection against the spread of fire.

In the event of a fire or other fault disabling either power car, the train can still continue to exit the Tunnel even if only two of the three motor blocs at the other end are functioning.

The brake system components have special protection against fire to ensure the train is not brought to a stand in the Tunnel. The passenger alarm handles within the vehicle saloon do not apply the brakes but instead alert both the Driver and Train Manager to the area concerned to allow them to take action as necessary.

Other Safety Features

Should it be necessary to stop the train in the Channel Tunnel in the event of an emergency, the Driver has the option to abandon part of the train by instructing staff to split the train from inside at any one of three places:

a) Between the power car and R1 trailer vehicle.

b) Between the power car and R18 trailer vehicle.

c) Between the two half-sets at R9 and R10 trailer vehicles.

Passengers can be transferred from one half of the train to the other in a well-rehearsed evacuation procedure. Should it be necessary to evacuate the entire train, passengers can be detrained into the adjacent Service Tunnel via one of the many linking cross-passages spaced at 375m intervals.

As part of the procedures prior to entry into the Channel Tunnel the driver is guided by a special indicator light on the cab desk. When not illuminated this informs the driver that all the safety systems and equipment necessary for transit through the tunnel are in working order.

Other safety systems include:

a) Instability sensors mounted on the bogies which instruct the driver to stop or reduce speed in the event of mechanical defect.

b) Wheelslide protection system to prevent the wheels 'locking up' under heavy braking (cf ABS on domestic cars).

c) Wheelspin protection system to ensure controlled application of power to the wheels to prevent them from slipping (cf traction control on domestic cars).

d) Laminated glass windows in the passenger saloon with toughened glass in diagonal corners with safety bar and 'break-glass' hammers.

e) Emergency equipment including ladders, signalling track circuit clips, equipment for isolation of the third-rail supply, hand tools, first aid box, conventional railway fog signals, flares and flags to warn approaching trains.

f) Data recording equipment, similar to the 'black box' on aircraft, which can be played back at a later date in the event of an incident.

The Three Capitals sets are not permitted to run off the designated Tunnel routes because:

- There is a risk of pantograph dewirement under BR's 25kV due to the dynamic loading gauge to which the trains were designed and for which the infrastructure of the CTRs was modified to accommodate
- Interference currents are not compatible with signalling track circuits

- The 500V dc auxiliary power supply is only returned via the running rails (NOL trains have return cables)
- NRN radio is not fitted
- Inadequate accommodation for Control Authorities on the trains
- The train length exceeds platform length except at Waterloo

Computer Systems

Three Capitals trains have 28 Programmable Logic Controllers connected to the network. The network is known as 'Informatique' (from the French for electronic data processing). Data is passed between the power cars and trailer vehicles for control of the traction and braking effort, status of control systems and equipment, passenger display information and alarms. The system is a more powerful version of the technology utilised on the TGV Atlantique. Although critical information is transmitted though the network software, all safety related circuits also have 'hardwired' equivalent systems.

Information regarding the status of the train is displayed in the cab and any equipment faults are logged so they can be downloaded by maintenance staff using a laptop computer.

Provision is made for a data radio system to be used to give maintenance staff advance warning of defects before the trains arrive back at the depot, and to allow remote pre-conditioning of trains (ie to switch the heating on by remote control when the train is stabled).

Signalling Interference Monitor

The train is designed to ensure that the electrical systems do not export currents above specified levels at the various signalling circuit frequencies and thus interfere with the track signalling systems. An Interference Current Monitoring Unit (ICMU) is fitted to both power cars which measures the levels of electrical interference produced by the train and ensures it does not exceed the safe limits of the routes over which Eurostar operates. The equipment includes the Ansaldo 50Hz detector for the 750V routes and the DT50 detector for use on the Belgian 3kV dc route. Extensive analysis was also undertaken which required the replacement of susceptible signalling systems prior to the introduction of the Eurostar service on the routes through southern England.

Above: The train cleaning plant at North Pole depot — part of Eurostar's commitment to quality of service.

Right: A TMST powered trailer.

North of London Trains

The length of Three Capitals trains prevents their use at stations served by the north of London services in Britain. To alleviate this problem, seven shorter North of London sets have been procured specifically for these services. These trains consist of two power cars and fourteen trailer vehicles, 320m in length, formed as shown in Table 1. It is planned that passport and baggage checks will be carried out on board the trains.

The North of London vehicles are equipped as shown in Table 2.

This gives a total train capacity of 558 seats of which 114 seats are First Class and 444 are Standard Class. The option to change either of the R7/R12 to smoking accommodation is available.

Other differences on the North of London trains include:

a) Addition of anti-roll bars on power car suspension system to limit deviation of pantograph from overhead wire when cornering at speed and in high winds.

b) Modification to Train Supply system to prevent return currents from flowing through the rails back to the power car.

c) Incorporation of the Adtranz Multi-frequency Monitor ICMU for protection of signalling systems north of London.

d) Larger accommodation for British Customs staff and portable security equipment.

e) Modification to permit compatibility of the 25kV pantograph developed for operation on the French high-speed line with the British 25kV overhead catenary system.

Overleaf: The best is yet to come . . . *BM*

Table 1
M1 + R1 + R3 + R2 + R5 + R6 + R7 + R9 + R10 + R12 + R13 + R14 + R17 + R16 + R18 + M2

half-set	half-set

Table 2

Vehicle	Class	Smoking	Seats	Toilets	Additional Facilities
R1/R18	2nd	No	48	1	Nursery/Family Area/ Baby Changing Facility
R3/R16	2nd	No	58	2	
R2/R17	2nd	No	58	1	Train Manager's Office/Telephone
R5/R14	2nd	Yes	58	2	
R6/R13	Buffet	No	-	-	Bar and Catering Area
R7/R12	1st	No	39	1	Relaxation Area
R9/R10	1st	No	18	-	Disabled Persons Area and Toilet Luggage Compartment/Telephone

Left: Following a scheduled stop at Ashford for electrical testing alongside a Class 92, Regional Eurostar set Nos 3307/3308 restarts and heads for North Pole Junction on 1 May 1997. *BM*